Key Words to Reading

The Language Experience Approach Begins

Second Edition

Key Words to Reading

The Language Experience Approach Begins

JEANNETTE VEATCH
Professor Emerita
Arizona State University

FLORENCE SAWICKI
Indiana University, Northwest

GERALDINE ELLIOTT

ELEANOR FLAKE
Litchfield School District
Litchfield Park, Arizona

JANIS BLAKEY
University of Alberta

CHARLES E. MERRILL PUBLISHING COMPANY
A Bell & Howell Company
Columbus   Toronto   London   Sydney

. . . What a dangerous activity reading is: teaching is.
All this plastering on of foreign stuff. Why plaster on at all
when there's so much inside already? So much locked in?
If only I could get it out and use it as working material.
And not draw it out either. If I had a light enough touch
it would just come out of its own volcanic power.

Sylvia Ashton-Warner in *Spinster*

To Sylvia Ashton-Warner

Published by
Charles E. Merrill Publishing Company
A Bell & Howell Company
Columbus, Ohio 43216

This book was set in English No. 49 and Oracle.
The production editor was Cherlyn B. Paul.
The cover was designed by Will Chenoweth.

Photographs on pages 2, 29, 114, 115, 118, and 212 are courtesy of
Joan Bergstrom. Photographs on pages 27, 84, and 132 are from
Resource Teaching (Merrill, 1978). Photographs on pages 18, 34, 39,
66, 67, 114, 170, 173, 177, and 204 are from *Values in the Classroom*
(Merrill, 1977).

Library of Congress Catalog Card Number: 78-61850

International Standard Book Number: 0-675-08363-X

1 2 3 4 5 6 7 8 9 10—83 82 81 80 79

PRINTED IN THE UNITED STATES OF AMERICA

Foreword

Teaching a child to read by individualizing instruction and utilizing his or her language and actual experience has many labels, many agreements, and still more disagreements. However, one basic concept is shared by all. Individualizing instruction by utilizing the child's actual experience is a reading approach rather than a reading method.

A reading method accepts the traditional reading program as it is and strives to predict teacher and pupil behavior. A reading approach requires the traditional reading program to change and prepares the teacher to effectively deal with pupil behaviors as they emerge. Obviously, a reading approach, if carried out effectively, will restructure present reading programs by changing the roles of administrators, teachers, and pupils.

I believe that *Key Words to Reading* can provide educators with information needed to change existing reading programs, because it grew out of the writers' actual experiences. They worked with administrators, teachers, and pupils in ongoing school situations. As they observed problems, they found ways to solve them. As they observed excellent techniques, they found ways to integrate them into this total approach. The outcome resulted in an excellent guide for educators.

The *key word* aspect of the well-established Language Experience approach is quite unique. The pupil is given the opportunity to acquire a personal collection of words. In turn, teachers use this psychologically sound learning opportunity for story-starting situations, motivating devices, and lessons in letter-sound–letter-form skill development.

If educators are in search of a lasting way to change present reading programs, they should being with *Key Words to Reading*—ultimately, it will help them depend on their own instructional leadership.

Nicholas J. Silvaroli
Director, Reading Education
Arizona State University

v

Preface

The approach to reading and writing called "language experience" has been with us for many years. The work of Laura Zirbes, R. Van Allen, Dorris May Lee, Virgil Herrick, among many others, has been noteworthy. Little did we know, when struggling to produce the teachers' guide (a forerunner of the first edition) privately with offset type, that the seeds of the practical application of what is now called the "psycholinguistic approach" were being fertilized. The first edition, which this replaces, offers the *how* of what professionals, such as Kenneth Goodman and Frank Smith, are currently writing about, and the *why* of children's own language and its value as instructional material. This concept is new. Although systematically derived, such language is spontaneous and contains the hopes, fears, ideas, and dreams of children. And this is powerful language indeed.

This book is written to present the basic idea that the language of children is full of tremendous possibilities. We have faith that such potential is human, not commercial, and that it lies in the hearts, minds, and souls of all children and all teachers. There are ways of getting at this gold mine of language; and that is what this book is all about.

It is written to present ways and means of eliciting children's dramas in language. It is not a canned package to be spoon-fed to every child from coast to coast—yet the language of the Hispanic American in the Southwest, the Black American in the ghetto, the Samoan in Pago Pago, and the white American in the suburb holds literary magic.

Research on all aspects of the language experience approach has long been needed. At this writing, interest in the British Primary School has resulted in publications entitled *Language for Life,* which says it all. In addition, Kenneth Goodman, Frank Smith, R. Van Allen, and Elaine Vilscek Wolfe have added to the riches in store for those teachers who view commercial reading systems as despotism of texts. May all this activity aid in developing the kind of society which earns the name civilization.

Out of all this, we hope that some clarification of issues between the "humanists" and "behaviorists" occurs. One will not find in these pages any stop to behavioral objectives. Instead, we stand on objectives and, in so doing, hope to yield some light on the differences between inner ideas as instructional material and imposed ideas that do not exist in a given learner's mind. This is the basis of the language experience approach—this is what the psycholinguists are trying to encourage.

Originally developed through a funded project in Chandler, Arizona, this book is one of the increasing number of contributions to these unique ideas. We hope that it continues the effort to assist teachers who value their pupils as thinking, talking human beings—human beings who have enough inside to keep us all busy for some time to come.

Acknowledgments

Since the teachers' guide appeared, several of the authors have moved to other areas of the country. Nevertheless, special thanks are still due to the administration and teachers of the public schools of Chandler, Arizona, which supported the initial project.

In the intervening years, the authors have continued to explore these and other aspects of the language experience approach. There are other teachers in other school systems who have experimented further, both formally and informally. Raymond J. Duquette deserves mention for his ongoing work at California State University at Bakersfield, which grew out of his work as one of the original investigators for our project.

We have abiding faith in the classroom teacher who strives daily to bring children to the seat of learning. May these individuals, wherever they are, know that we love and respect them as much as our original inspiration does from her home "down under."

The Authors

Contents

Key Words to Reading

The Language Experience Approach Begins

Second Edition

1

The Beginning

No matter what method or system a teacher might use to help children begin to read, one miracle must occur or flat failure will result. That miracle is the realization by the beginning reader that *I have words in my head!* For such is the stuff of literacy. This accomplishment is so powerful that it provides all motivation necessary to set children's feet on the path of learning, and yet it is most easily discovered as it naturally exists within the learner. It is the awareness that what has been thought is right there, available and in words. These words have no pictures with them, for pictures are not needed; they are already in the mind. This is the essense of the great contribution of Roach Van Allen, and teachers and children alike should be eternally in his debt.[1]

Learning to read and write is a process that should be as natural for children as learning to walk or talk, for it is simply a higher level of the imitative process. But it is not an instinct and it does require instruction. How the teacher approaches this instruction is particularly important if she[2] wishes to preserve the child's natural enthusiasm for learning. Most children are anxious to start school, and indeed, most of them love their first- and second-grade teachers. But by the middle grades, something

---

[1]R. V. Lee and R. Van Allen, *Learning to Read through Experience,* 2nd ed. (New York: Appleton Century Crofts, 1963), chapter one.

[2]In order to avoid awkwardness of dual pronouns (for example, "he or she"), the authors and editor have alternated chapter by chapter the use of he and she in reference to students and teachers.

3

happens to their enthusiasm. Why? It is the incessant, perpetual demands of imposed tasks, usually irrelevant to any interest a child might have. This is what is meant by the tyranny of textbook learning. Using textbooks to the exclusion of language experience—especially in the beginning—sets up a despotism in the teacher-centered classroom. The teacher who is terrified at the thought of allowing children to use their own language becomes one who dares not depart from those sacred pages, the printed lesson, and prevents learning from coming from the inside out.

Because such teacher-centered, publisher-centered curricula are usually the cause of disinterest in learning, we propose to describe teacher-pupil interaction on a systematic, organized, and planned basis. This is the only way to develop content with the merit of being original with the pupils, and therefore exciting to them when developed into instructional activities. We feel that the writings of Sylvia Ashton-Warner are among the best to help teachers use students' inner ideas and words as instructional material. She is the driving force behind this entire presentation. From the solid base of *Spinster* and *Teacher*,[3] we offer an expanded approach to such beginnings.

Using Ashton-Warner's work as a base, we will describe in as clear a manner as possible the how, what, and wherefore of helping children along the path to literacy.

Classroom Environment

Let us begin at the beginning—the physical environment of the classroom. Before children come to school, a teacher needs to prepare their classroom for them. Decisions on how the desks should be arranged, what needs to be displayed, and where things will go are all questions teachers face at the beginning of every school year.

Arrangement of classrooms depends greatly upon a teacher's philosophy. But whatever the teacher's philosophy or whatever the physical arrangements provided by the local board of education, there are certain things that we feel must be in all classrooms, regardless of how big, how self-contained, or how open-spaced they might be (see figure 1).

There should be enough wall space to hold five pieces of 2' × 3' newsprint paper, one for each day of the week. As each day passes, the teacher will copy the morning's pupil dictation in the best of manuscript and post it on the wall so that any child anywhere in the room can look up and see these "newspapers." Figure 2 shows how such a wall might look.

[3]Sylvia Ashton-Warner, *Spinster* (New York: Simon & Schuster, 1959); idem, *Teacher* (New York: Simon & Schuster, 1963).

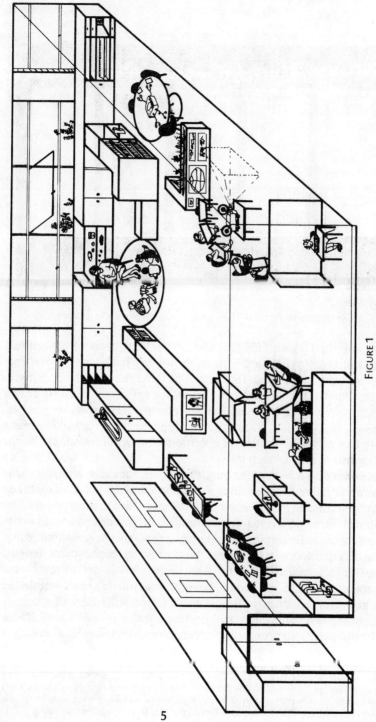

FIGURE 1
One example of classroom layout

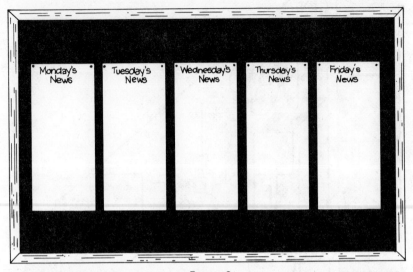

FIGURE 2
The posted daily news sheets for ready reference by students

The authors feel strongly that one of the best pieces of educational equipment is the chalkboard—black, green, or what have you. We urge that it be kept clean enough for free use by the children as the class hours run on. The beautiful thing about a chalkboard is that it allows one to make mistakes. What a fine ego builder for a new learner working on new learnings! If it's wrong, erase it, and nothing lost. There should be many square feet of chalkboard in all classrooms, and children should be encouraged to use them freely![4]

Somewhere on a wall, at the pupils' eye level, should be alphabet cards as shown in figure 3. These cards should be about $9'' \times 12''$ so that they can be seen from anywhere in the room. As described in chapter three, the pupils will learn how to incorporate the alphabet in learning how to write.

Perhaps our main message is that a classroom must have wall space that is practical and *used*—no frilly bulletin boards, no teacher-made designs, no spelling papers with "100%" on them. This is not to say that a classroom must not have color, beauty, or aesthetic appeal—quite the contrary. The test of any classroom, and especially the wall space, is whether or not a pupil will be stopped in his tracks to take a look. There can be no better criterion for evaluating physical settings in school.

---

[4]One author observed a "chalkboard" in Hawaii. But washable ink, not chalk, was the writing medium, and the board was of a material that a wet sponge would clean. This seems like a good idea until one realizes that the high humidity of Hawaii (and many other places) does not allow the ink to dry rapidly. Therefore, the use of such a board is limited to the few minutes each message must take to dry. Result? No one wrote much on that board.

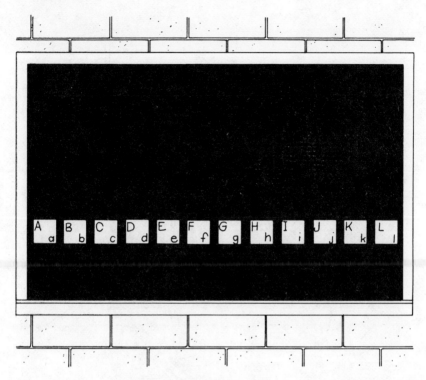

FIGURE 3
The alphabet at pupils' eye level

Another part of a classroom must allow enough space for the entire group to sit cross-legged in an audience situation. This is particularly important when the teacher is leading a dictation for the day's news. Perhaps the teacher is beside an easel or close to a chalkboard. But there should be space for all children to watch the dictation that comes each morning. If possible, seats might be moved so that children can sit comfortably on their own piece of floor. Figure 4 depicts such a session.

Although we hope that the environment of a classroom using the language experience approach is different from that of a teacher-centered, textbook-oriented one, wide variations are certainly available. If the reader wishes to reflect on this point, scan chapter five to see how many centers of interest are possible. The point is that the classroom setting should provide for relevant, reality-based experiences.

The average classroom is not likely to resemble the child's home, yet it is important to remember that, for several hours a day, the classroom *is* his home. For this reason, activities that take place in school should facilitate learning by means of life-relevant incidents. For example, a post

FIGURE 4
Taking dictation

office set up in a classroom might be successful in motivating letter writing, but many real life opportunities for children to write and mail real letters would be better yet. Writing letters to living people is a life-related activity for it uses the child's language and life experiences. Thus, the classroom arrangement should provide a variety of opportunities that will allow children to engage in activities freely and spontaneously in groups or individually, yet at the same time, it should provide for instruction.

Teachers and lay people are dreadfully confused about the need for instruction. Free play is an instinctive activity. It does not require instruction. But reading and writing *do* require instruction even though such instruction *may be based* upon free play or another life activity (such as eating, having a picnic, and the like). Understanding these differences clarifies the distinction between laissez-faire and spontaneity, yet allows for a philosophy wherein learning requires teaching.

Classroom Organization

Although children are not as easily distracted as teachers may think they are, classroom organization is nonetheless extremely important. The placement of desks and tables should allow traffic to and from supply centers and group and individual sessions with the teacher to be as direct and noninterruptive to other pupils as possible.

A classroom should be organized so that opportunities for the following major activities can be offered:

1. Individual conferences with the teacher
2. Group conferences with the teacher
3. Whole-class, audience-type activities
4. Independent individual activities
5. Independent group activities

Chapter five, Independent Activities, includes a detailed discussion of classroom management. All of the above activities can easily fit into any average classroom. The important idea for the present purpose is to help the reader visualize the various types of activities that transpire in a classroom. Each of the above activities will be further elaborated upon in the following chapters.

Workbooks and Teacher-made Exercises

The philosophy of this text is built around instruction that uses the child's own living experience. Therefore, exercises designed to keep children busy without real educative value are not encouraged.

An exploration of the literature on the value of workbooks and worksheets will reveal that they are practically worthless in terms of learning. Agatha Townsend's discovery in "Workbooks—The Research Story"[5] is not the only finding to reflect their lack of educative value. It is most unfortunate that such exercises are *demanded* by thousands of teachers. Even those principals who would wish it otherwise feel helpless to deny their teachers such tools. According to Sylvia Ashton-Warner:

> Teachers say they need their workbooks.
> They say, "I can't rely on myself in the melee of a lesson to work out sequences on the spot. When the time comes I need everything at my fingertips. I've got to have it all thought out beforehand. . . . "

---

[5]Agatha Townsend, "Workbooks—The Research Story," *The Reading Teacher* 17 (February 1964): 397.

I know that the preparation of a workbook may clarify to a teacher what he is thinking about. I know that the order and method of it reflect inescapably upon the minds of the children. And I suspect from what I see that the very fact of a workbook evokes on the mind of a teacher a reliable peace. And that its notes mean that necessary steppingstone between his conception and his execution. Indeed, I can believe comfortably enough that the assessment of a workbook can be truthfully close to the assessment of a man. It is neither the fact of a workbook nor its phase in teaching that is the point of departure. It's the incorrigible variety in man himself.

For some teachers just don't see a workbook in this way. True, they see it in the same place between conception and execution but not as a steppingstone. To some teachers the workbook is the middle man intercepting some of the energy and glamour directed upon the canvas. Leonardo da Vinci cut straight into his marble. Rabindranath Tagore wrote his verse neat and I didn't hear of Jesus making notes. Teachers, all of them in one medium or another, who mistrusted the middle man.

To the extent that a teacher is an artist . . . his inner eye has the native power, unatrophied, to hold the work he means to do . . . he would rather risk a blank in his teaching than expend cash on the middleman . . . He wants to see in his mind, as he teaches, the idea itself, rather than the page it is written on. He wants to work . . . directly upon the children without interference from the image of its [the idea's] record on the book. He wants to work in a way that to him is clear, without conflict, and without interception.

It doesn't always, I think, clarify a teacher's thoughts to note them down . . . when in teaching I found that I was required to preceed all my work with the written notes of the workbook, it was with gross payment to the middle man that I did so.

In an infant room, however, where activity is wholly expressive, with all subjects allowed their legitimate entry into the area of creativity, the question of a workbook can hardly arise. Wherever there's creativity on a large scale, there's life, and I, anyway, can't plot life. I just join in. How are we to know what is going to come from the children on this day or that? How can I tell what the reading and spelling is going to be since each morning they write their own books for the day's use? Does a teacher wish to anticipate the purposes of each new day? In an infant room cultivating the organic expansion, a teacher learns to put the factors of mood and change before the prognostications of a workbook . . . not the professor but the artist is the true school master.''[6]

Agnes De Mille says, in much the same way:

. . . Living is a form of not being sure, of not knowing what next or how. The moment one knows how, one begins to die a little . . . the artist be-

---

[6] Ashton-Warner, *Teacher*, pp. 88–90. Reprinted by permission of the publisher and author.

fore all others never entirely knows. He guesses. And he may be wrong. But
then how does one know whom to befriend or, for that matter, whom to
marry? One can't go through life on hands and knees. One leaps in the
dark. . . . [7]

These two artists, each in her own way, have written about the excitement of seizing upon spontaneous expression. "Leap in the dark!" says
Agnes De Mille. But how many teachers can? How many dare? Those
that can and dare are those that can live with the uncertainty of what
words a child may give them, of what books a child might choose to read.
Easy? Not always. Exhilarating? Yes, because the teacher who needs no
artificial middle man to give her the next question, and the next, and the
next, knows her own strength.

But there are many who dare not move out on their own or who say
their principals will not let them. These teachers, then, at all costs must
keep their classes reasonably tidy and in order. No matter what, children
cannot be allowed to be chaotic, and the teacher cannot be violent
towards the children. As someone has said, "You can hold 'em but you
can't hit 'em."

So, assuming that no reader *really* needs help in using workbooks, let us
proceed to other activities that can be done by pupils independently.
Teachers are not needed by the students, at least not *all* the time. With
proper use of independent activities, teachers are given the freedom to instruct individuals or groups. The secret to independent activity and, in-
cidentally, to the independent learning of which the workbooks can never
boast, lies in the setting up of *interest centers*. The whole of chapter five is
devoted to independent activities; this chapter will provide the necessary
suggestions for teachers who, while working with an individual student,
do not know what to do with the rest of the class unless they use workbooks.

Getting Acquainted in School

When the teacher meets her class for the first time, and her classroom setting suits her, she should begin by getting acquainted with the children
before starting to use any of the activities found within this text. Reading
initially comes from the child's own language, although he also should be
hearing good literature read aloud. In order for a teacher to capitalize on
the child's language, she must first develop a relationship with the child. If
a child does not feel comfortable in school, he will not talk to the teacher

---

[7]Agnes De Mille, *And Promenade Home* (Boston: Little Brown and Co., 1958), p. 190.

or to anyone else; therefore, *the first meeting should start by getting acquainted.*

The Need for Talking

The approach to reading and writing described in this book uses a child's own speech and provides experiences that are closely related to the child's personal and social needs. Thus, through the use of the child's oral language, he learns to read and write. Speaking is the most fundamental skill of the language arts and should already have developed spontaneously in the preschool years. A genuine interest in children and a respect for their oral contribution on the teacher's part builds the child's self-concept. This acceptance and understanding of each child in turn helps him to feel at ease, confident of success, and able to master those fears and tensions that block expression.

The silent classroom is the deadliest of instructional atmospheres. The teacher who is convinced that noisy children are a direct threat to her authority deprives those children of the interaction which is crucial to their development as literate humans. The curriculum of such a classroom cannot be based on the child's needs and interests. In fact, a silent classroom denies the chance to use speech as a learning tool. Enough has been written about the crushing totalitarianism, whether benevolent or not, of the teacher who permits talking only on her own terms. The best teachers know how to handle talking without losing control of their children. No one wants a raging, disorganized, chaotic class, but the teacher who knows how to use speech to enhance learning is a better teacher than the one who clamps down on children's urges to communicate with each other. Classrooms need not be silent, nor do they need to be uproarious. Speech, talk, and communication are major resources of the teacher which she can use in many ways.

Thus, there are many dimensions to the language experience approach. These dimensions have never been better stated than in Lee and Van Allen's *Learning to Read through Experience.*[8]

What he thinks about he can talk about.
What he can talk about can be expressed in painting, writing, or some other form.
Anything he writes can be read.
He can read what he writes and what other people write.

---

[8]Lee and Van Allen, *Learning to Read through Experience,* 2nd ed., chapter one.

As he represents the sounds he makes through speech with symbols, he uses the same symbols (letters) over and over.

These aspects are abbreviated from a more detailed list but can be cited justly by all as the skeletal framework of the language experience approach.

We might simplify Lee and Van Allen's list in the following manner:

1. The teacher gets the children to talk spontaneously, probably in a group or whole-class situation.
2. Some or all of the talk is written down by the teacher.
3. Activities of myriad sorts in talking, reading, and writing are developed.

What we insist upon is that the teacher must use the children's own speech and either provide experiences or utilize those that arise spontaneously to fill the child's own personal, social, and academic needs. It is through the use of the child's oral language that he learns to read and write. Speaking is the most fundamental skill of the language arts, and it is certainly one of the most impressive accomplishments of the human being prior to his fourth birthday!

This development, which occurs largely as a function of the home, provides riches for the use of the teacher in developing literacy. On the other hand, a child who is inhibited in speech presents this problem as the first major challenge to the teacher. Speech must be developed. Sylvia Ashton-Warner has said of this situation, "The conversation has to be got."

A classroom that encourages and *manages* the expressions of ideas, that allows each child to feel that his speech is important, that institutes ways of "taking turns" is the classroom that builds stronger egos and better literate skills.[9] As was previously noted, a genuine interest in children and a respect for their oral contributions on the part of the teacher builds the child's self-concept. The teacher's acceptance and understanding of each child help him to feel at ease and confident of success. Indeed, confidence, as Ruth Strickland has pointed out, is the "memory of success."[10]

The language experience approach cannot be mechanized. It is perhaps the only noncommercial program that is humanistic in character. For the purposes of this book, we see the activity called "key vocabulary" as being an adjunct of such an approach. This approach clearly is useful at the beginning stages of reading and writing and undoubtedly has some valid-

---

[9]See chapter seven for results of research of Barnette, Duquette, and Packer.

[10]Ruth Strickland, *The Language Arts in the Elementary School* (Boston: D.C. Heath and Company, 1965).

ity with older age levels (with minor adaptations in deference to the older age group). We see it as initiating the whole process of reading and writing. It is a beginning that precedes sentence dictation; it is a logical outcome of the small child's scribbling on paper. Our definition of the language experience approach is inclusive of early babbles and scribbles before the child arrives in school.

Getting Children to Talk

Children need to be able to communicate verbally in order to have a successful experience in reading or writing. But getting children to talk is not always easy; some children are very verbal and will need little encouragement while others will need *something* to talk about. It is the teacher's job to chair the talks rather than to lead them.

There are many ideas and stories inside the mind of a child. These ideas are the stuff out of which words are born, for from these ideas come words that have a meaningful impact on the child. They are what he knows so he knows how to read them, and he reads them because he wants to and not because he has to.

The teacher creates a feeling of relaxation by sitting down and talking with the group. Once everyone is reasonably relaxed and feels free to express himself, the teacher is on her way to eliciting a key word from each child. The teacher may find it best if the day starts by getting a key word from each child while it is fresh in his mind. However, many times a child simply has no key word in the morning so the teacher must wait and be hopeful, helpful, and encouraging. Sooner or later, one word will come or *many* words will come—sometimes in a flood.

The manner in which the teacher organizes the pupils can have an effect. Sylvia Ashton-Warner suggests groups of eight children at a time. Some teachers like to have independent activities or quiet free play going on, with the children wandering in from the playground as they wish, until the school day is to formally begin. A teacher should try out various ways of eliciting words, in a group or one by one, or however it seems easiest and most effective. Here are some suggestions that can work well for eliciting key vocabulary, and just as well for the whole-class dictation of the day's news.

1. Ask personal kinds of questions: "What did you do before you came to school?" "How did you get to school?" "Where do you live?" "What do you like?"
2. Present pictures to class: "What do you see happening in this picture?" "How do you think this person feels?" "Why do you think she looks like that?"

3. Make plans for the day: "What would you like to do today?" "What should we do first, then what?" "What would be lots of fun to do today?"
4. Talk about the children's feelings: "How do you feel about going to school?" "How do you feel about helping your parents at home?" "What do you think about the weather?"
5. Talk about events: "What do you think about the accident that happened yesterday?" "What do you think about the new building going up across the street?" "How do you feel about the milk strike?"
6. Talk about trips: "Where did you go this summer?" "Has anyone been to a zoo?" "What is your favorite place?"
7. Talk about people: "Who is your favorite person?" "Whom do you like the best?" "Who is the most helpful person you know?"
8. Talk about activities: "What do you like to do?" "What is the most exciting thing you have done?" "What would you like to do?"
9. Play games that involve some kind of talking: "Simon Says," "Seven Up," "May I."

Guidelines for Using the Key Vocabulary in the Classroom

Here is a simplified set of guidelines to use in obtaining key words. Greater detail is to be found in the next chapter, but these suggestions may be helpful for now.

Elicit the key word from each child. Ask children questions like "What is the *best* word you can think of—or the scariest word—or the nicest thing?" Accept all words. If you doubt that the child is giving you a word of real power ask, "Why do you like that word?" Then let your conscience be your guide. The more powerful the word the better.

Print the word on a piece of tagboard (about 8" × 11") with a black marker or crayon. Have the child tell you the letters he recognizes as he watches you print. (Have him stand by your shoulder so that he does not look at the word upside down.) If he does not recognize the letter, say it as you print it. Refer him to the alphabet on the wall.

Have him trace your printing with his finger. Say something like: "As if your finger is my marker—" and watch only to see that he makes the left side of the letters before the right side and that he goes from top to bottom.

Send him off to write the word, draw a picture of it, copy it on the blackboard, or do SOMETHING with it.

*Once in a while (perhaps every other day) have each child bring his
words to you to say them as fast as possible.* Those he cannot recognize
instantly must be thrown away without criticism. "Oh, that just wasn't a
good enough word to remember. You will think of a better one today or
tomorrow."

Summary

This first chapter has dealt with beginning measures for using informal,
open-structured activities leading to literate children. Classroom environment was described in its basic, humanistic terms. The place of instruction
as contrasted to a laissez-faire approach was discussed, and the need for
spontaneous talking urged. The language experience approach was clari-
fied and defined, and the place in which the authors see key words was
presented in detail. Finally, some thoughts on the inadequacies of workbooks and their use, as well as an explanation of independent activities,
closed the discussion. The chapter proposes to pave the way for a teacher
to read on and develop a classroom utilizing these ideas.

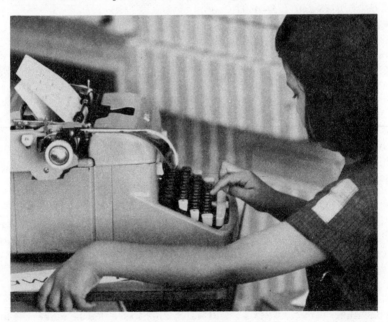

FIGURE 5
Finding the keys for the key words

2

Key
Vocabulary

The first moment a child comes into a classroom she has within herself words that have meaning and feeling for her. She does not need a reader of any kind to tell her things that she already knows, or a teacher whose vocabulary contains words that have no meaning for her. It becomes the teacher's job to try to release the child's meaningful words and record them for her eyes to see, her hands to write, and her mind to read. For it is the mind that does the reading. The eyes are only the windows for the brain. "For this reason, attempting to speed up the rate of fixation from the four or five . . . normally made [by] a reader is a pointless endeavor since the information bottleneck is in the brain."[1] The value of the language experience approach is that it provides a means of allowing the mind to read, because the mind uses its own thoughts as substance. In this text we are suggesting the activity "Key Vocabulary" because we believe it to be the fastest and most effective way to get the acts of reading and writing underway.

The value of key vocabulary is what Sylvia Ashton-Warner discovered one day in her Maori classroom. Her discovery was not something that just happened; rather, she had been looking for this for some time, although she did not know it until the day one of her students asked her

[1]Frank Smith, "Some Limitations upon Spoken and Written Language Learning and Its Use," in *Children with Special Needs,* eds. H.H. Spicker, N.J. Anastasiow, and W.L. Hodges (Minneapolis: Leadership Training Institute/Special Education, University of Minnesota, 1976), p. 41.

how to say the word "kiss." The moment she told the child the word, there was a reaction that she had never seen before. Upon hearing the word, the child smiled, his face lit up, he grabbed the book and ran around showing the word "kiss" to all of his peers. The reaction did not stop here—before she knew what was happening, all of the children were reading the word "kiss," talking about the word "kiss," and writing the word "kiss." The word "kiss" might not be a word with which a teacher wants to start teaching reading—but it is a kind of word that begins reading. This type of word is said to make up "key vocabulary" because it is the type of word that, once expressed, opens the mind to reading what the eyes see.

Key Words: A Keystone

To more than one reading specialist, the introduction of key vocabulary words presents the keystone in the arch of reading. In a sense, it completes the total instructional program. While many professionals have believed in and used pupil dictation in what was usually called the "language experience approach," there still has always been the nagging question of how to ease the very young child into reading instruction. *Key vocabulary* provides that initiation into the world of literacy.

Unfortunately, the authors of many reading programs did not understand and certainly did not agree with this new concept when it was introduced. They believed and proposed program after program of sight words that were to be *put into* the child by means of incessant drill, reinforcement, or exhortation, under the guise of "motivation."

The Arrival of Spinster

In 1958, a novel crossed the ocean to America which electrified thousands of teachers and offered a new approach to reading instruction. One read it, if a teacher, with mounting excitement and awareness that "I am truly a warm, loving human being. I have fears, hopes, weaknesses, loves. I am *Human!*" One read it hungrily, if a teacher, and regretted when it was done because it simply could not be started all over again with the same sense of fulfillment, the same feeling of being mirror-imaged in a way that even Hollywood cannot imitate very well. The novel was *Spinster* by Sylvia Ashton-Warner.[2] It found a home on the best seller list as well as in

---

[2]Sylvia Ashton-Warner, *Spinster* (New York: Simon and Schuster, 1959).

the secret heart of practically every school teacher who read it. It was chosen as one of the top ten of the *New York Times* Best Books of the Year. Inevitably, it was issued in paperback. *Spinster* was the kind of a book people enjoyed sharing with their friends.

Two Major Effects.   *Spinster* had two major effects that are of concern to this text. First, it was the first best seller that drew the portrait of the school teacher in human terms. There have been other books, but not such big sellers. Second, it presented to reading teachers an innovation of such unique proportion that many teachers still do not know—or, if they know, do not truly understand—the nature of the gift. This innovation is, of course, the concept of *key vocabulary.*[3]

The Need for More on Key Vocabulary

The initial success of *Spinster* led its vast audience to demand more of the same. The publishers were inundated with letters. Ashton-Warner was the delighted recipient of hundreds more. The recurring theme of these letters was "tell more about key vocabulary." In due time came *Teacher,*[4] albeit a text, but one of the most eloquent and charming texts budding teachers ever had the good fortune to read. Where *Spinster* had told *what, Teacher* told *how.* It transported the reader again into the infant school room of Ashton-Warner and helped that reader visualize what this type of teaching was all about. It did such a good job of projecting this infant school room on to the screen of the reader's mind that the practice of key vocabulary came to be tried in many parts of this country. It was tried stumblingly, perhaps, but *it was tried. Key vocabulary* became the pass-word for a huge fraternity of creative teachers. The book became a standard item in college and university book stores—even in those schools which offered only the most meagre of teacher-education programs. Both are still on the standard reorder list in such places.

The Gift of Sylvia Ashton-Warner

The following extact from *Teacher* contains the words that started the movement for key vocabulary. They tell what this book is all about.

---

[3] We italicize this phrase to indicate that it has special meaning that we will define and describe. By the use of italics, we intend to designate a specific kind of vocabulary.

[4] Its author later confessed it had been written long ago, but, lacking a publisher, had to wait for the success of *Spinster.*

First words must have an intense meaning.
First words must be already part of the dynamic life.
First books must be made of the stuff of the child himself,
whatever and wherever the child.

The words, which I write on large tough cards and give to the children to read, prove to be one-look words if they are accurately enough chosen. They are plain enough in conversation. It's the conversation that has to be got . . . if it can't be . . . if the vocabulary of a child is still inaccessible, one can always begin him . . . (with) . . . a set of words . . . associated with the inner world: "Mummy," "Daddy," "kiss," "frightened," "ghost."

"Mohi," I ask a new five, an undisciplined Maori, "what word do you want?"

"Jet!"

I smile and write it on a strong little card and give it to him. "What is it again?"

"Jet!"

"You can bring it back in the morning. What do you want, Gay?"

Gay is the classic overdisciplined, bullied victim of a respectable mother.

"House," she whispers. So I write that, too, and give it to her eager hand.

"What do you want, Seven?" Seven is a violent Maori. "Bomb! Bomb! I want bomb!"

So Seven gets his word "bomb" and challenges anyone to take it from him.

And so on through the rest of them. They ask for a new word each morning and never have I to repeat to them what it is. And if you saw the condition of these tough little cards the next morning you'd know why they need to be of tough cardboard or heavy drawing paper rather than thin paper.

When each has the nucleus of a reading vocabulary and I know they are at peace with me I show them the word "frightened" and at once all together they burst out with what they are frightened of. Nearly all the Maoris say "the ghost" . . . while the Europeans name some animal they have never seen, "tiger" or "alligator," using it symbolically for the unnameable fear that we all have.

"I not frightened of anysing!" shouts my future murderer, Seven.

"Aren't you?"

"No, I stick my knife into it all!"

"What will you stick your knife into?"

"I stick my knife into the tigers!"

. . . So I give him "tigers" and never have I to repeat this word to him, and in the morning the little card shows the dirt and disrepair of passionate usage.[5]

---

[5]Sylvia Ashton-Warner, *Teacher*, p. 35. Reprinted by permission of the publisher and author.

Challenge to Tradition

Since the traditional approach to reading was material-centered, it is surprising that *Spinster* and *Teacher* aroused such an out-sized response
among teachers, let alone among the population in general. Reasons for
this have not been researched, but it seems clear that these two books said
something to the American teacher that could not be found in the usual
text on the teaching of reading.

Ashton-Warner's book, *Spearpoint,* relates more than the *what* and
how of key vocabulary.[6] It described some of the present-day influences
in the United States that work against the child-influences that may in-
hibit the elicitation of key words. Ashton-Warner points out that some of
the stumbling blocks in eliciting powerful key words may be related to our
present-day society and its attitudes about children. In a most sensitive
manner, Ashton-Warner describes how she overcame these stumbling
blocks. She outlines the "records" she kept, the observations she made,
and the material she created. *Spearpoint* gives a clear picture of what
Ashton-Warner terms an "organic classroom"—a classroom that brings
together living and learning.

Each of her books presents a description of a relationship of the child
with her teacher. Each book showed that children's own words from their
own minds were the best words to start them on the long hard task
towards literacy—towards reading and writing.

These are the single-concept words Ashton-Warner called "captions of
mind pictures"; they make up the core of the key vocabulary approach.
Key vocabulary for the first time offered American teachers an approach
that was concerned about the child's "mind picture"; the nation's
reading programs had never been built upon any innate child's imagery.

Suffice it to say that *Spinster* and *Teacher* set something in motion that
was new and different on the educational horizon. It showed teachers how
to teach reading and writing without lists of sight words. Interestingly
enough, though, the basic idea was not new; for literally centuries,
teachers have known that the child's own interests make possible the
greatest motivation for learning. What was new was the interest and excitement engendered by a new source.

---

⁵Sylvia Ashton-Warner, *Teacher,* p. 35. Reprinted by permission of the publisher and
author.

⁶Sylvia Ashton-Warner, *Spearpoint; Teacher in America* (New York: Alfred A. Knopf,
1972).

Recently there has been suggestion that these elicited words—so unexpected, so spontaneous—are analogous to Piaget's sensori-motor, preoperational, and concrete operational stages. He went so far as to say:

Teaching means creating situations where structures can be discovered. . . .
Words are probably not a short cut to understanding; the *level of understanding seems to modify the language* that is used rather than vice versa.[7]

To underline the importance of this analogy, Copeland[8] discusses the pre-operational stage in terms of representation as a beginning of language. "The word 'tree,' for example," he says, "is not a tree but a symbolic representation of 'tree'! . . . The use of symbols or 'representation' marks the beginning of thought. . . . "

Precisely. As thousands of teachers have discovered, and as Hartman[9] is researching, there is a correlation between the ability to classify, in Piagetian terms, and the stages of learning to read. The quality of thought of a very young child, when giving the teacher a key word, is startlingly similar to the reaction of a child who discovers that the same amount of water will fill a tall vase or a squat vase.

We are suggesting, then, that the miracle we mentioned earlier—*I have words in my head!*—can in no other way be better developed than by eliciting those words and writing them down for all to see. The unexpected nature of the words elicited and the predictability of their importance to the child represent a psychological, cognitive, and perhaps even physical element which merits intensive exploration. In due time the psycholinguists may have more answers than are now available. The Piaget of reading has yet to be identified. Nevertheless, Sylvia Ashton-Warner, in writing her first novel, hit upon a kind of magic that will keep educators busy for some time to come.

Developing Key Words

We see key vocabulary as an initiating event on the path to literacy. It may be just one of several activities using children's own language, or it may be

[7]Eleanor Duckworth, "Piaget Rediscovered," in *Readings in Science Education for the Elementary Schools,* eds. Edward Victor and Marjorie S. Lerner (New York: Macmillan Co., 1967), pp. 317–319. Emphasis added.

[8]R.W. Copeland, *How Children Learn Mathematics* (New York: Macmillan Co., 1970), pp. 13–15.

[9]Thomas Hartman, "The Relationship Among the Ability to Classify Retrieval Time from Semantic Memory and Reading Ability of Elementary School Children" (Ph.D. diss., Memphis State University, 1977).

the prelude to the language experience approach. The one-word–one-look-word concept is, of course, a component of basic sight vocabulary, and sight words are necessary to beginning reading, for they can serve as a spring board into talking and writing.

In the early stages of development, some children do not always understand the one-word concept of key vocabulary. If a child is asked to give her "best word," she may say, "I love my Mommie." To her, the entire sentence is her "best word"; it is all one mass of sound, and she cannot separate it into units. In such a case, the teacher's role becomes that of a true facilitator of learning. He asks the child, "Who else do you love?" As the child responds, "I love my Daddy," "I love my puppy," etc., an extremely important process is taking place: the child is developing *interchangeability* in her use of language. By interchanging parts of her language, the child can see that her thoughts are made of separate units which adults call words. Sooner or later, she develops the ability to select one word from a thought. However, even when the child can see the interchangeability of words, whole sentences should be recorded, because many skills can be taught through such spontaneous speech.

As soon as possible, the teacher should move children from speaking into story-writing. This is done by simply encouraging children to put "other words" with their key word. Sentences of two, three, or many words soon develop. From such sentences, the teacher can move children into story-writing by saying "What else can you say about your word?" The child thus moves from single, one-look words to sentences, and from sentences to pages, and on to the ultimate achievement of the writing of her own books. As real authors, children come to understand best what authorship means.

The movement from key vocabulary into longer pieces of writing is so simple that many teachers are not aware that a change has taken place. Student dictation and individual writing energizes the more mundane "service words" as well as developing key words. Filling out ideas into pages and stories is a logical development. Key vocabulary enhances and simplifies the language experience approach.

Key vocabulary is a very simple, but extremely powerful technique. As one principal said, "It *can't* be that easy!" But it is, because it sets in motion an intense motivational force—intense, because it comes from within the child herself. Therefore, the child becomes self-directed and the teacher's role is reversed. He is no longer a supplier of information but, rather, a facilitator of learning.

In the Vancouver project Ashton-Warner and Wasserman[10] formalized these stages, referring to them as "movements." For example:

---

[10]Selma Wasserman. *A study of the Key Vocabulary Approach to Beginning Reading in an Organic Classroom Context* (Vancouver, B.C.: Board of Education, 1975).

First Movement (key vocabulary)

1. Child's "best" word is elicited.
2. Child's word is whispered in teacher's ear. (variation: Teacher-pupil conversation is held, out of which the teacher chooses what he feels to be the "best" word.)[11]
3. Print the word on a large card.
4. Have child trace the word.
5. Enter into conversation with child about the word (different conversation from that in #2).
6. Have the child *do* something with her word.
7. Review word next day; words not remembered are discarded.

Second Movement

1. A two-word "caption," for example, "new puppy," is elicited.
2. A smaller card is used.
3. Smaller print is used.
4. Repeat appropriate steps above.

Third Movement

1. Child will give more words, phrases, and even sentences. (However, phrases and sentences are not to be identified as such.)
2. Small books are used to record words. (Move from unlined paper to wide lines, then to narrower lines. Books start with a few pages and each subsequent book gets thicker.)
3. Usually by the third book, the child is writing her own sentences and short stories, and needs very little teacher help.

Fourth Movement

1. Child's writing becomes much more sophisticated.
2. Child has acquired sufficient skills to read commercially published books, and is now ready for a self-chosen, individualized reading program.

Van Allen's recent text[12] concurs to a great extent with these observations of developing movement patterns. Yet surprisingly he omits any mention of key vocabulary as presented by Ashton-Warner. We believe this weakens an otherwise superb methodology.

---

[11]These authors are not convinced this is a viable alternative to the guidelines that follow. The suggestion is offered because some might find it useful. We pointed out that each letter need not be named as it is printed, and feel this is a serious omission.

[12]R. Van Allen, *Language Experiences in Communication* (New York: Houghton Mifflin, 1976).

Basic Steps of Obtaining Key Vocabulary Words

The procedure for obtaining key words is quite simple. The child tells the teacher the words she wants, and the teacher records it for the child to see, saying the letters as he writes. The child then traces the word with her finger; finally, she writes it. Thus, the key word begins its task of unlocking the words in the child's mind and leading directly into the reading process. It is an activity that truly begins "with the child where she is."

Probably the simplest and most common way to sabotage the effectiveness of key vocabulary is for the teacher to be unwilling to accept the child's word. Any reluctance at all—a sharp glance, a change in the tone of voice, or simply an unsmiling face—can convince the child that this is not really her game. Once this occurs, key vocabulary is no better than any other teacher-oriented, teacher-planned program. To make this program work, the teacher must convince the child that the entire program belongs to her and that her experiences are singular and unique.

Sylvia Ashton-Warner took the concept of "interest words" from one aspect of her own teacher training in New Zealand and developed it to fit its present form. The child and what she thinks, rather than what an adult deems to be important, make up the vital part in the interest word concept. If a teacher can reach into a child's mind and find the words that

.FIGURE 6
Learning words with a partner

have real meaning to her, reading will take place within a short period of time. This task, in essence, is the first job of a teacher. That is where it

Words obtained from conversation with the child are unique because they come from the child's personal life. Even more exciting from the standpoint of the teacher is that these words are acceptable and desirable for use in reading instruction *in school*. Thus, the outside world of each child is brought inside the walls of the classroom—living becomes a part of learning, and learning becomes a natural part of life.

Guidelines in Detail

The following guidelines were those used by the experimental teachers in the research study discussed in the preface to this volume. Other teachers may approach the same activity in a different way, but the crucial points are that only the children's own words are taken and that, later on, those words that are not remembered are thrown away.

Elicit a Key Word from Each Child.   The word a child gives must have an emotional impact for her; otherwise, it will probably not be retained. The teacher tells the class that he wants them to tell him their favorite word, one that makes them feel happy, sad, or angry, or one that is funny or scary. The children should be asked questions like, "What is the best word you can think of" or the "scariest word" or "the nicest thing." All words should be accepted. If the teacher doubts that the child is giving a word of real power, he can ask, "Why do you like the word?" He should then let his conscience be his guide. The more powerful the word is, the better.

Print the Word on a Piece of Tagboard.   Each child now whispers her word into the teacher's ear. This is a technique that adds intrigue to the activity for some children, while providing a security factor for shy children. In time, most children will discard the "whisper technique" naturally.

The teacher then writes the word on a large (perhaps 8½ " × 11 ") card with a felt pen or crayon. While the teacher is writing, the child should stand by his shoulder so that she does not see the word upside down. The children then name the letters they know, and the teacher tells them the ones they don't know. Thus, the process of letter identification begins. If the child does not recognize the letter, the teacher can say it as he prints it.

Let the Child Trace the Word.   The child should be allowed to trace the word with her finger. The teacher, meanwhile, checks for left-to-right and

FIGURE 7
Closeness between children and teacher

top-to-bottom direction on the child's writing. He immediately corrects
any handwriting errors or reversals. This practice also affords the child an
opportunity to feel her word as well as name the letters.

The Child Does Something with the Word.   The child is now sent off to
write the word, draw a picture of it, copy it on the chalkboard, or do
something with it (see activity section at end of chapter). The activity is of
her own choosing and may include such things as painting a picture of the
word, writing the word on the board or on individual chalk slate, writing
other words about her word.

Review Words with the Child.   Once in a while (perhaps every other day)
each child brings her words to the teacher to say them as fast as possible.
Those she cannot recognize *instantly* must be filed away without criticism. The teacher should make a remark like, "Oh, that just wasn't a
good enough word to remember. You will think of a better one today or
tomorrow." Words the child does not remember are not significant to
her. No attempt should be made to "teach" any word.

Storing the Words.   Storage of the words soon becomes a problem.
There are several ways this can be handled:

1. Individual folders can be used.
2. A ring file can be made by having the children punch holes in their word cards and place them on a shower curtain ring or metal ring, in alphabetical order or at random.

These are the bare bones of the key word activity. Much can be done to enhance and develop this and other aspects of the approach known as *language experience*. What follows fleshes out these bare bones and is designed to help teachers understand this approach.

Activities Extending Key Words

Group Activities

1. *Retrieving Words from the Floor.* The children's words (usually the words of a group or of half the class are best) are placed on the floor face down. On the signal, each child is to find her own word, hold it up, and tell it to whoever is watching.
2. *Claiming the Cards.* The teacher selects many words from the class, holds them up, and the child who "owns" each word claims it.
3. *Telling Stories Spontaneously.* The child attempts to tell a story about her word. The story does not have to be recorded; she should be allowed to make it up as she goes along.
4. *Classifying Words.* Certain kinds of topics—for example, desserts, television characters, funny words, places, scary words—are chosen. Topics are selected according to classification. All of the children who have a "dessert" word, for example, would stand in one spot. The teacher might want to label the spot with a sheet of paper that says "dessert." Children who have words of other classifications also stand in their designated areas.
5. *Relating Words.* One child might have the word "cake," and another the word "knife." In such a case, a child might say that a knife can cut a cake. The teacher should try, somehow or other, to get the children to relate the words through such questions as: "What can my word do to the cake?" "How can my word be used with the cake?" "Is there something that my word can do with the cake?" The teacher can continue this by asking the children, "Does someone else have a word that can be used with the word 'cake'?"

6. *Exchanging Words.* An exchange for discarded words works wonders. If a child does not know his word, the teacher replies, "That doesn't make any difference. Just put it in the exchange box." Children may go through the exchange box any time and if they find a word they want and *know,* they may take that word to add to their stockpile. If they lose a word and cannot find one to replace it, they may get another one from the teacher.

7. *Learning a Partner's Words.* Each child chooses a partner, and they teach each other their own words.

8. *Coauthorship.* Two or more children can get together and combine their words or ideas to make longer and longer words or stories about their original words.

9. *Using Two Words in Story.* Children work in groups of two. Each child selects one word from her stockpile of favorite words. She then uses the two words to write a silly story, a funny story, a sad story, or a make-believe story.

10. *Pass-it-on Stories.* Children select words from their piles of words. For example, they might select such Halloween words as "haunted," "night storm," "owls," "bats." The teacher lists several categories on board or chart. The first child in a group will write the title; the next child, the starting of the story; each child in the group adds something new to the story. (A group should be composed of no more than five members.) One child should be selected to read the finished story.

11. *Acting Out Words.* If the key word is conducive to "acting out," the child can sometimes dramatize her word for the others to guess. Examples are "rabbit," "owl," "bird," "clock," "Indian."

12. *Hiding Word.* The word is written on medium-sized piece of heavy paper (perhaps 4″ × 5″). When children are at recess, the teacher puts the words around the room in easy-to-spot places. In various ways, children thus get their words.

Individual Activities

1. *Making Booklets.* The teacher can make a booklet of words and pictures. The booklet should be designed so that when it is open, both the picture and word can be seen at the same time.

2. *Making Alphabet Books.* After children are sure they know their words and can claim them for their own, the words are recorded in the correct section of an alphabet book that is divided by initial letter.

3. *Making Sentences*. The children write their words on a piece of paper or on the chalkboard and then proceed to add other words, such as service words, to make sentences of varying length. The following are some examples of sentences written for key words: Get the *lion*. Casper, the *ghost*, can fly.
4. *Illustrating*. The child can draw a picture about the key word, then dictate a caption for the teacher to write on it.
5. *Making Jigsaw Puzzles*. The teacher can write the child's key word on a piece of newsprint or cardboard, then cut it into three or more pieces for the child to reassemble. Or, the teacher can write the key word on a piece of cardboard, and the child can paste or draw a picture on the other side. The teacher can then cut this into pieces for the child to reassemble.
6. *Simple Clay Sculpting*. With a small portion of modeling clay, the child can shape words or objects in connection with the words.
7. *Circling the Clue Words*. Children are encouraged to look for and circle all the clue words they can find in the printed column. They then count these words, tell the class how many words are circled, and name a number of the words.
8. *Grouping Illustrations*. The child can pick out six or more favorite words from those on the ring, then make a booklet of illustrations for these words.
9. *Making Books for Each Child*. The teacher staples a quantity of lined writing paper on each side of the interior of the book. The left side is used for each day's key words. The child can then illustrate, write a sentence, or story about her word.
10. *Painting Words and Pictures*. The children paint their words and paint pictures to illustrate their words.
11. *Typing Words*. The child writes her words on the typewriter, magic slate, or chalk slate. She can also use magnetic letters or flannel letters.
12. *Writing Words*. The child can write a word on paper or on the chalkboard.
13. *Finding Words*. The child can find a word in a book, magazine, or newspaper.
14. *Writing Words with Fingerpaint*. The child dips her finger in fingerpaints and writes her word.
15. *Tracing Word on Felt*. Using a large piece of felt, the child makes her word and traces on felt with her finger.
16. *Writing in Sand or Salt*. With her finger, the child writes the word in salt or sand.

17. *Making Word with Masking Tape.* With masking tape the child forms the letters of the word on the floor of the classroom and traces it with her finger.

18. *Writing Key Word in a Sentence.* When writing a key word in a sentence, the child will use a different colored marking pen to write the key word.

19. *Glitter Word.* The child can write out word with white glue on paper and sprinkle glitter, sand, or fine gravel. Shake off the excess.

20. *Stencils.* The child can use stencils of various letter styles to trace words.

21. *Giant Words.* The child can blow-up the word with an opaque projector to get a giant-sized word image.

22. *Word Cookies.* The child can write the word with cookie dough, then decorate, bake, and eat.

3

Writing

Story writing is a necessary part of the key vocabulary program. In this program, anything the child writes is accepted. Comments, good or bad, and corrections are never put on a paper, for as soon as a child feels an evaluation has been made of his writing, it ceases to be his and comes to belong to his teachers.

The children would feel free to speak without fear of being evaluated. In this context, neither punishment nor reward, represented by high or low grades, makes any sense. Evaluation focuses their attention on approval and not on exploring their ideas.

A teacher who insists on perfect spelling, micrometer margins, and neatness—in fact, a teacher who *insists* on anything—will get "What I Did Last Summer" and "We Should All Be Good Citizens" essays, because insisting is just the thing not to do if you want someone to tell you how *he* feels. The more rigid the requirements, the more rigid the writing.

Discipline in writing can be a good thing if it is imposed from within. First the children need to see what it is like to really think on paper.[1]

The Bullock report is eloquent about the development of language that becomes writing. It advocates that visiting nurses instruct young and new parents,

---

[1] Stephen M. Joseph, ed., *The Me Nobody Knows* (New York: Avon Books, 1969), p. 10. Copyright © 1969 by Stephen M. Joseph. Reprinted by permission of the publisher.

When you give your child a bath, bathe him in language . . . Most nursery and infant teachers recognize that when young children are involved in some activity, the talk that accompanies is an important instrument for learning. It is fed by nursery rhymes and singing games, by the stories that teachers and children tell and the poems they read . . . the teacher introduces the written language. What it brings is fresh material to be talked about, *for the spoken word must mediate the written.*

Eventually these spoken words become words that are printed for and read by the child. As the Bullock report describes,

By degrees, beginning with the words he already knows, the child will take over the writing until the whole caption is his own work. The "books" are collections of such pages. The child reads his sentence back to his teacher, and in this way this personal collection of captions and sentences becomes his first reading book . . . Captions or labels of use and interest to the children are often to be found in the classroom . . . as reading proficiency increases, there will be no longer always the same need for pictures.[2]

We do not want to leave the impression that great and wonderful growth will occur without some systematic and well-organized intervention into children's language. As advantageous as it may be to have as many adults as possible interacting with small children, we believe that interaction must involve oral response to definite questioning. In short, the interaction cannot be one-sided. The problem is a misinterpretation of this type of interaction by overconscientious teachers who literally hound children to repeat a phrase correctly. As one boy said to such a person, "I don't want to talk anymore." And he didn't.

Genuine, honest interchange of ideas between an adult and one or more children will enrich the soil of language development. Repetitive drill on speech errors will dry it out to a desert. If there seems to be a fine line between intervening and drilling, perhaps there is; but the continual enthusiasm of the child is a criteria. We reject laissez-faire use of experience. We applaud the following uses of language, and urge that records be kept of progress.

Reporting on present and recalled experiences.
Collaborating towards agreed ends.
Projecting into the future; anticipating and predicting.
Projecting and comparing possible alternatives.
Perceiving causal and dependent relationships.

---

[2]Alan Bullock, *Language for Life* (London: Her Majesty's Stationery Office, 1975), pp. 14, 22. Emphasis added.

Giving explanations of how and why things happen.
Expressing and recognizing tentativeness.
Dealing with problems in the imagination and seeing possible solutions.
Creating experience through the use of imagination.
Justifying behavior.
Reflecting on feelings, their own and other people's.[3]

Writing and Reading Are Inseparable

Thus, in the primary classroom writing should be thought of as a part of reading and not as a separate activity; reading and writing are learned together. We read what others have written. The child should discover at an early age that he must be able to write if he wants someone to know what he feels and thinks. As a matter of fact, children write (early scribblings) and *know what they mean to say* before they read.

FIGURE 8
Making the letters just right

---

[3]Bullock, *Language for Life,* p. 30.

The writing ability comes from awareness, as the child sees and reads what a teacher has recorded during the classroom talk. From that, the move is made to a written record of his own words for others to read. The teacher helps and makes provisions for a child to release his writing ability.

The fact that the child is not already a good writer when he enters the classroom for the first time is not the point here. The point is that—whether it be good, bad, or indifferent—the child has the writing ability within him. Although teachers worry about improving the ability after the child has shown what his ability is, worrying about teaching the basic skills of writing is not the place to begin. The child learns to write by writing or copying.

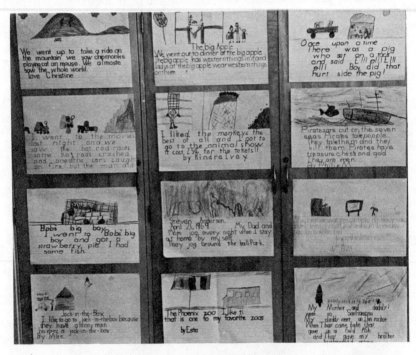

FIGURE 9
Sharing each story with the class

How Writing Teaches Reading

The crux of this section is the belief that writing, *by its very nature,* is an analytical skill or ability. Therefore, the sooner a child can write independently, the sooner he can read independently. Once the writing ability is acquired, the problem of decoding words in reading is simplified.

Spelling and Reading

Spelling is a skill that allows a child to hear a word that he cannot see or visualize. When a child writes or traces a word, as suggested in the guidelines in chapter one, he *sees* it; therefore, he is *reading* it just after he has finished writing it himself or watching his teacher write it for him. All adults recognize the act of "seeing if it looks right" when they themselves write. This is an excellent example of how writing feeds into the act of reading. When children—or anyone else for, that matter—are writing something, they are writing an already encoded set of words. Thus, the writing, an automatic decoding operation, teaches the reading, in that writing teaches the child to decode so that this decoding skill can be used in a different situation.

The discussion about decoding and encoding is related to writing down words that are said. "Talk written down" is a common phrase used to describe the language experience approach. The point is that when a child says a word he wants to write, he is saying a word that is already *encoded*

FIGURE 10
Reading her story to a friend

in his mind; the decoding operation then is easy. As clarification, one might think of assembling a jigsaw puzzle; it is much easier to assemble when the person working on it has seen the picture on the cover of the puzzle box. Seeing that picture is literally an encoding operation, and having it to refer to while putting the puzzle together makes the entire project easier.

This discussion of writing illustrates another of the philosophical differences between teaching reading with teacher-imposed content and teaching reading with child-chosen content. The choice, in effect, facilitates the *encoding*. Again, once a child says a word that he wants to write, he is well on his way to recognizing it (that is, reading it) when he next sees it. The teacher's role in this process is not to tell the children what to write, but to provide means by which to discover words. If she is successful, the children may become so involved in their writing that they won't want to do anything else.

Instruction in phonics and reading skills is a natural outgrowth of the child's writing. The child learns the skills as he needs them and when he needs them. The succeeding areas of instruction will develop naturally and with very little formal instruction.

Mechanics of Spelling and Writing

Spelling is useful for writing and nothing else. Too many teachers give children the idea that spelling is only for the Friday test, although this approach raises havoc with the intrinsic principle that learning is a valid goal, in and of itself. When children are taught to recognize that various letter sounds in the alphabet are the same as those found in their own words, they can then learn how to begin to write other words which have some of the same sounds as the words they already know. It may be that in the first instance the child can only record the first and last letter. A line indicating missing letters will do for that moment or until the teacher is able to help the pupils with the mechanics of hearing and seeing sounds in the middle of words. It is conveying the idea on paper, not the word itself, that is of immediate importance.

In this way, the child's skill in writing and reading increases. The child can then go off on a spree of writing at any time. Once he can copy key words, he has acquired enough skills to begin to write—with a little help if needed.

Spelling rules, if taught at all, are taught as they are seen in the written word. The use of rules—especially *before* their application—is an unmitigated waste of time and interest. Very few are even useful, and these we note learned and relearned on into adulthood; "*I* before *E,* except after *C*" is one. We suggest that the best way to learn to spell is by writing the letters that are heard in a word (see page 69) and omitting those that are not heard. For example, in the word *from,* we hear the *f,* the *r,* and the *m,* and we must *remember* that the third letter is an *o.* But to *hear* 75 percent of any word will sharply reduce the need to *learn by heart.* Spelling is greatly simplified if pupils are taught to hear. And hearing, in turn, is simplified by the use of the *names* of letters in the alphabet rather than their sounds, which are pure gibberish and indeed difficult to recognize by hearing.

Hearing letters leads to the use of invented spelling which, in defiance of nearly every commercial spelling program on the market, is necessary to the growing capability of children to handle more complicated learning situations. Phonetic and invented spelling are quite proper in the early stages; when a pupil can read back from his paper, "Hpe brthda, mthr," he is well on his way to becoming a literate person in a short time. Because he does not have to memorize an entire word without a rationale to guide him, he can *hear* the letters that are obvious and then memorize the very few elusive ones. Later on, such practice works wonders on the lists of spelling words that are thought to be helpful if learned *in lists.* Of course, they aren't.

In short, spelling rules are taught as the need arises. The child, in writing his first stories, is not expected to know how to spell each and every word. In order not to discourage writing, the child should be allowed to spell each word the way he hears it.

The phonetic rules learned in this approach are not rules that are taught as a separate activity; rather, they are rules that are learned through one major activity—the written language of the child.[4] Once the child knows a word, he can begin to discover certain relationships among the words used in his language. In this manner, the teacher can help a child learn certain phonic rules when the need arises rather than when the rule first appears in the workbook.

Penmanship in the Language Experience Approach

One of the observations we made while developing key words was the importance of the way letters were made in relation to the child's ability *to read back what he had written.* The definition of legibility is, of course, the ability to communicate to a reader through the hand-written word. It

---

[4]Nevertheless, the discussion of phonics in chapter six does describe how phonics lessons can be established.

was obvious to us that children need to be taught how to make their letters, and we found that children need to be taught fairly consistent letter forms.

But how is this direct instruction to be carried out? Look again at the guidelines in chapter one and remember that once a word has been elicited from the child, it is written down by the teacher on a tough piece of tagboard while the child watches. As the child watches, he identifies the letters that the teacher is writing—usually, printing. In the *next* step, he traces over the letters he has just seen his teacher make. *The teacher watches his tracing very, very closely; this is the act of learning to write in direct instructional terms.*

FIGURE 11
The partial-circle method

The Partial-Circle Method

The teacher should be aware of three main characteristics of this method:

1. All round letters are made by the partial-circle method.[5]
2. Tall letters and short letters are clearly tall or short (see figure 11 for examples of these features).
3. Directions are, for the most part, from left to right and from top to bottom (except *m* and *n*).

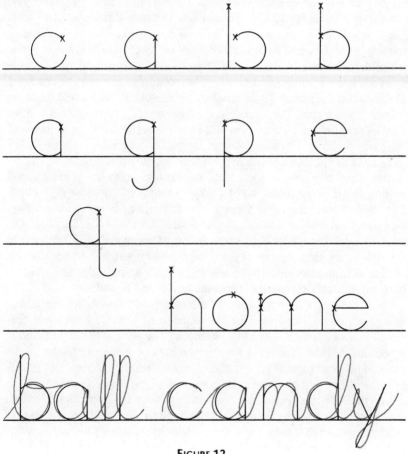

FIGURE 12
The evolution of cursive writing

---

[5]The only exception is *o*, of course.

These three features of the partial-circle method facilitate the change to cursive writing which occurs late in second grade or in third grade. Figure 12 explains this graphically.

From a brief look at these transitional phases, it is clear that the partial-circle method more easily converts into cursive writing because the starting points of each letter are at what might be called the "ten o'clock" and "two o'clock" positions. For example:

Although research studies may be lacking, our experience in working with hundreds of teachers verifies to our satisfaction our belief that children taught by the full-circle method start their letters in the wrong place for easy conversion to cursive writing. The peculiar retracing of line patterns shown in figure 12 is a familiar one to many third-grade teachers. The "two o'clock" partial-circle method establishes the "two-o'clock" starting point of round letters, and it is not easily changed as time goes on.

Children trained in the full-circle method may *begin* all right, but it takes intensive teaching and constant correction to prevent the changing of the beginning points (designated by an *x* in our illustrations) from the proper "two o'clock" position to the improper "twelve o'clock" position.[6] The more coordinated the child becomes, the faster he writes, and the more certainly this shift of starting position becomes ingrained—as thousands of third-grade teachers will mournfully attest.

This text presents a total reading-writing program—reading and writing merge in the recording of a power word (key word) for each pupil. The child thus receives direct instruction in writing, as well as in reading, on a one-to-one basis. This is not meant to imply that a teacher might not want to teach the whole class some aspect of penmanship; it is meant to say that every child, every day will be carefully watched to see that his writing continually follows the left-to-right direction, goes from top to bottom, and uses the partial-circle method on all round letters.

Many readers will recognize that the tracing element is not something new; a touch of Montessori and a soupçon of Fernald have been borrowed in developing it. Even one portion of *The Writing Road to Reading* by Spaulding and Walter[7] is used in the idea of using the hands of the clock. The reader should not think, though, that the authors' use of one portion of any system constitutes approval of the entire system.

To conclude this section on penmanship, we wish to emphasize clearcut instruction without confusion. Every pupil who watches the teacher write his word for the day, and then, under the teacher's watchful eye, is able to trace that word, does not need formal drill in order to learn to

---

[6]These children also tend to move from the "ten o'clock" position to the "twelve o'clock" position as illustrated in the letters *b* and *p*.

[7]Spaulding, Romalda and Spaulding, T. Walter, *The Writing Road to Reading* (New York: Whiteside, Inc., and Wm. Morrow and Co., 1962), p. 74.

write. But penmanship is more than writing—it is legible, even aesthetically pleasing writing. The partial-circle method is so simple that one would almost expect legible handwriting to come naturally, although of course this is not the case. And this is where pride of achievement enters the picture. When a pupil says to his teacher, "Isn't that the nicest *g*, Ms. X?" he is letting us know that he has acquired the valuable habit of writing legibly and handsomely. We believe that children must be taught to write just as they must be taught to eat with knives and forks; but such direct teaching is easier, faster, and more lasting when it is based on the need to communicate.

Taking Dictation from Children

Stories have to have a beginning, although the beginning could be just one word said by a child. In this section, the "one word" is a unit of thought which Sylvia Ashton-Warner calls a *key word*.

As children talk, the teacher records key words on the board. Key words are the main thoughts or ideas of the conversation. If a child says, "Mike learned how to ride my bike last night," the teacher would write the word *bike* on the board. This technique allows the conversation to continue, but if the teacher tries to record everything the children say as they say it, the flow of talk is sure to be broken.

Once the key words are recorded, they may be read by the children or the teacher. The children then give a sentence about each key word. This is another advantage of the key word technique: children may be able to recall an entire idea from a single word clue. It is like a spotlight on a single thought or idea.

The topics of the experience stories formed by children's sentences are endless. Other stories may have different topics, but the steps used in writing any story are usually the same. These steps have been summarized in the following way:

1. As children talk, the teacher listens and records a key word on a piece of paper. This procedure permits the flow of talk to continue in an uninterrupted manner.
2. The teacher then writes the key words on the chalkboard. She keeps in mind the child who initiated each topic and checks that the key words selected do, indeed, relate to the topic.
3. The teacher writes a sentence on the board that captures the child's idea. As she writes, she tells the children what she is writing and asks them if it is what they want to say.

4. Manuscript writing, rather than cursive is used. Not only is it easier to read, but also it resembles the printed symbols found in books.
5. Continue the story until it reflects a "wholeness of content"—until it seems finished.[8]
6. After class time, the teacher makes a permanent copy of the story on a clean sheet of durable paper.
7. The story chart should be placed on a chart rack or in a place where children can refer to it when they desire.

The story should not be written for the class to see just once and then forget. After writing a story, the teacher can try any of these suggested activities:

1. The teacher may need to read the story to the children in the initial stage of the language experience approach.
2. Some child in the class might read the whole story by himself. A child learns quickly when reading something that has real meaning for him.
3. The teacher can ask individuals to find certain sentences in the story and read them aloud.
4. Once the children can find certain sentences, the teacher can have them look for phrases in their stories by using both hands to block off the phrase that a child is reading.
5. Children can find rhyming words or words that "begin like your name."
6. As phonics skills increase, children can find words with short vowels, or digraphs, or other specified phonetic elements.

These daily experience stories are reservoirs of language—and it is language of the children. Some editing is needed: pupil dictation with wrong usage is altered, and the wrong word is found and changed. Good English must be used in all instructional material; hence the teacher must listen to make necessary changes in that direction, while taking care not to obliterate the unique and often charming language that the class has offered.

Of all the language available to teachers, there is hardly a richer source than the excited talk of a group of primary children. Develop, encourage, and preserve it.

---

[8]One question often asked about experience stories is, "How long should they be?" There is no set rule to answer this question. The length of the talking and writing period will depend on the attention of the children. As soon as the children get restless, a change of some kind is needed.

Acquisition of Service Words

Service words are those words that do little to produce a picture in the mind. They *serve* to glue the language together. These are the hard-to-learn words, such as *the, was, saw, about, there*. Traditional readers get in trouble because these kinds of words occur so often in the language of the readers. In these cases, the words, essentially meaningless in themselves, are necessary to accent and give definition to the nouns and verbs that carry mental pictures and action with them. As the word count in readers is sharply restricted, authors who are not creative writers to begin with rely on the extensive repetition of *the, from, and*. Such a strategy makes a bigger book, but it also makes a duller book.

A quick glance at the story "The Baby Birds" (figure 13) will show that it contains 36 words. Of those, eighteen or fifty percent are of the type we call *service words,* incorrectly called *sight words*. Herein lies a strength of the language experience approach, in that those words usually meaningless, usually presented in the most sterile of instructional patterns, can be taught in normal ongoing speech-written-down. As we suggest, they are learned in their natural habitat of language that has come from the pupils. When talk is written down, the service words are read as they have been spoken. But although recognition is not easy, the context simplifies the acquisition of these words, for in most experience stories developed between teacher and pupils, service words make up about forty to sixty percent of those words dictated. This is the value of experience stories for the gaining of a sight vocabulary of service words, and it is in sharp contrast to the primer approach in which service words can only be gained by a drill method.

Keeping Daily Stories

To use the dictated material to best advantage, a teacher should begin the day with an account derived from the show-and-tell, general opening discussion, or talking time. This story can be written on a chalkboard or easel and later transferred to more durable material for *posting* on the wall. Should these experience stories disappear after they have been dictated, written, and read back, much of value will be lost.

Each day a general story, in which all children have participated, should be placed on the wall. Once in clear view, each day's story can be used, along with the preceding ones from that week, as a kind of reference work for children to use when they need to spell—particularly when they need to spell service words. It would be very rare indeed to have a week's supply of wall stories and not have most of the frequently used service words somewhere in the sentences. Once these stories are on view, the teacher can refuse to help a child spell such a word, but can say "Go look at Monday's story. The word you want is in it. I can see it from here!" Because they see service words in a meaningful context, children will be able to understand the need for them and will learn them more easily.

Another delightful practice is for the teacher to duplicate each day's news on notebook sized paper. Then, on Friday, the five days' efforts are stapled together, perhaps with a title page, to be carried triumphantly home. There is hardly a better way to convince a doubtful parent, suspicious of other than the hard-core basal reader approach, that learning to read is going very well indeed.

An Example of Writing an Experience Story

This is how one teacher developed an experience story with a first-grade class. A bird had built a nest under the eave outside the classroom window. The children had observed the activity from the building of the nest to the hatching of the eggs. Excitement ran high the morning the children arrived at school to find four baby birds in the nest. The stage was set to develop a reading lesson evolving from a real life experience. A lively conversation followed, and the teacher recorded caption words and responses on the chalkboard.

> "There are four baby birds in the nest!"
> "Their eyes are shut."
> "Where is the mother?"
> "They don't have any feathers."
> "What do they eat?"
> "How did they get out of the eggs?"
> "Look! One has his mouth open."

Teacher: Let's write a story about the birds, O.K.? What shall we call our story?

Child: The Baby Birds. (Teacher writes title.)

Teacher: What shall we say next?

The Baby Birds

We watched a mother bird build a nest.

The nest is outside the window.

The mother bird sat on the nest for a long time.

There are four baby birds in the nest.

FIGURE 13

Child: The baby birds hatched.

Teacher: Is that the first thing that happened?

Child: No, first we watched the mother bird build a nest.

Teacher: What do you want me to write?

Child: We watched a mother bird build a nest. (Teacher writes.)

Teacher: Where is the nest?

Child: The nest is outside the window. (Teacher writes.)

Teacher: What shall we write next?

Child: The mother bird sat on the nest for a long time. (Teacher writes.)

Teacher: What happened next?

Child: There are four baby birds in the nest now.

Suggested Follow-up Exercises

Word recognition and vocabulary development:

1 . Find the word that means make. *build*
2. Find the word that means young. *baby*
3. Find the word that means observe or look. *watch*
4. Find the words that tell where the bird built her nest. *outside the window*
5. Find the word that is the opposite of short. *long*

Phonetic analysis:

1. Find the word in our story that rhymes with best. *nest*
2. Find the words in our story that start the same way as boat. *bird, baby, build*

Structural analysis:

1. What letter tells us that there is more than one bird? *s*

Sequence:

Cut the sentences into strips and place them in the chalk trough. Have the children find the sentence that tells what happened first, second, third, fourth, and so on.

Moving Towards Independent Writing

A teacher continually strives to help children become independent in their writing, for there is simply not enough time in the day to spell every word for every child. In order to lessen the amount of time the child must spend in spelling individual words, the teacher should provide "helps" around the room. As we described earlier, children should be encouraged to spell as much of the word as possible, then draw a line for the rest of the word. The teacher can then help the child with the part he doesn't know. Only when the child feels he doesn't know any part of the word can he ask a friend or the teacher.

At first, as few as two, three, or four words can comprise a story. Entire pages cannot be expected in the beginning. Once a word has been spoken by a child, and he has watched his teacher write it and has read it back, he is free to try his hand at writing that word with as many others as make sense. For example, one child said, "bike"; he later wrote "bike riding."

From one word, language is developed into the written counterpart of what the child has had in his head in normal spontaneous conversation since he began talking. Sometimes a child—even at age six—will state that a whole sentence is one word. For example, a six-year-old told his teacher, "My dog ran away." No matter how hard that teacher tried, she could not help the child to understand that this statement was made up of four words. The child insisted that "My dog ran away" was his key word, and in his mind, the sentence was a *single* word.

A similar case occurred when a mother asked her three-year-old for "the best word in the world." The response was "Boots are made for walking," which was the title of a popular song at that time and, obviously, a favorite of the child. When the mother persisted, "Yes, but give me ONE word. You said five words!" the child spunkily replied, "What's the matter? Don't you like my word?" From these and many other instances, it can be seen that children think in thought units. They don't know it and would be utterly confused if told so, but when their "single word" can be placed in multiple-word sentences reflecting the natural spontaneity of the child's language, then the path to learning to read through writing is almost guaranteed.

Some teachers, as an intermediate step from the traditional readers, will take the children's key words and write stories *for* the children. This practice eases up somewhat on drilling on sight words, the standard practice for reading instruction with primers, but it is and should be *only* an intermediate step. In addition, we have some doubts as to the value of the time spent on writing original books that have *not* been dictated by the children, even if the stories are composed of the children's words.

Classroom Management for Writing Times

When writing time becomes a regular part of the classroom day, it might prove helpful to both children and teacher to talk about and agree upon a list of rules. The list can be placed somewhere in room for easy reference, or copies can be made for children to keep in their own desks.

Children need to see some kind of working organization in the class-room, and rules developed with children are more meaningful than those that are imposed upon them. Such rules might include: "Don't disturb your friend when he or she is writing a story," "Wait your turn for help from teacher," "While waiting for help, keep on working," "When teacher is free to help you, go back to the trouble spot." These rules are helps that free a teacher for teaching rather than policing.

We have found that teachers, made secure by a classroom full of pupils writing away at a furious rate, are loathe to teach any lesson that will in-terrupt the activity. The project teachers involved in the research for this book gradually stopped sequential teaching of any portion of the reading curriculum. Some eased off sooner than others, but most were so de-lighted with the obvious independence of their youngsters that they were satisfied to teach only what was needed when it was asked for.

Developing the Story Writing

It is important to remember that children have stories—loads and loads of stories. They are simply looking for someone to tell these stories to, and the teacher can easily be one of these people. She can become the vehicle through which the child can tell many others his story.

The teacher's role now changes from that of one who writes single words for her children to that of one who writes their stories. In essence she becomes a secretary writing out the dictation of her students. Now, when children come to her, they come to tell a story that will be written on a piece of paper. This paper is theirs, and they may do any one of a num-ber of things with it.

Punctuation

Contrary to some educators, we state that punctuation cannot be effec-tively taught silently; it is a function of voice inflection. A child automati-cally uses his voice meaningfully, so to tell a child to "read with expres-sion" is sheer teaching incompetence. Once a child has written his own ideas, he knows how they sound as he has said them, either silently to himself, or aloud as he wrote. Thus all of the important sounds that lead to punctuation are there for instructional use. No rules needed—no rules taught.

FIGURE 14
Working on those unknown words

Because the child knows what he tried to say in his story, the voice inflection should give him clues to where to place the comma, the period, or the quotation marks. As linguists have pointed out, it is not the words so much as the voice and its inflection that give meaning. To a surprising extent, words can be either virtually unintelligible or can convey much meaning depending upon vocal inflection. Thus, oral language once again leads the way to instruction; we learn punctuation and grammar from speaking and from listening to speech.

Let us elaborate on our idea that punctuation is an auditory activity. If a child cannot *hear* a sentence begin or end, he will never be able to understand what a teacher means when she says, "Put a period at the end of each sentence." But if punctuation is taught in the context of an auditory game, the child will master the skills quickly. For example, a child is allowed to read his story to the class. As he reads, the children listening pretend that their index fingers are pieces of chalk going forward to make a dot on an imaginary piece of paper. The children are to accompany the making of each dot with the clicking of their tongues. As soon as a story with a question is read, the children are asked if the sentence sounds the same as those preceding it. They will discover, on their own, that the reader is asking something in this sentence. So they are asked to make a question mark with their fingers. The same technique will work for a comma, which is only a pause, not a true stop.

A similar graphic way to teach the hardest of punctuation marks, the quotation mark, follows basic understanding of what punctuation really is—an expression of thought. As children are writing their stories, letters, or whatever else they may have chosen (and punctuation is *always* best taught through children's independent writing), the teacher says something like this:

In your story, if you have anyone saying anything, put their mouth around their words. You know how comic strips have balloons coming out of the mouth of the one who is speaking? This is just like that. Whenever anyone says any words, draw their mouth around those words—and just those words—to show that they did come out of the mouth.

After some experience in this process, so that the teacher can see that the concept of encircling spoken words is clear to the child, she can say:

Now you seem to have caught on to how to show the words people speak. Now let me show you the easier way to do the same thing. Take only the little corners of that big mouth you have been drawing and put the little smile marks with them so that you have two little curved marks that show that someone said something. We call those two little marks "quotation marks."

At first, the teacher will need to lead the children in this activity, but will soon be able to fade out and eventually discontinue the oral teaching of punctuation. The work can be resumed when a new type of punctuation is needed.

Capital Letters

The teaching of capital letters is a natural outgrowth of oral punctuation. The children may be told that they've learned the "stop signs" and now need to find the sign that lets them know it's time to "go" again. The "go sign" is, of course, a capital letter. They can also be told that people and places are important and need capital letters as well.

Spelling

Children are anxious to learn the rules of reading and writing once they see that it's worth their while. If a writing experience is worthwhile, then children will be anxious to learn how to spell. Rules are taught as the need arises. This technique will be discussed fully in chapter five, "Skill Development," but the following example will serve as an illustration for now.

Three six-year-old children were recently observed in a key vocabulary class. They needed the word "dangerous." Two of the children said, "It's spelled 'd-i.' "

"No," said the third. "Da-da-dangerous."

"Oh, you're right," and they write, "Day."

"No! That doesn't look right, it's just 'd-a.' "

"Hey, you're right. I just used that word in one of my stories. Let me find it—you go ahead and work on it. I'll be right back."

By the time the little girl returned, the two boys had written "dangierus" and had achieved an intermediate step toward perfect spelling! Thus, three children working together on a problem had spelled the word incorrectly, but were able to immediately accept the correct spelling from a child. The point is that they were truly interested in the "correct" way to write the word. They were not trying to please the teacher; they were trying to please themselves. They had experienced the ultimate of learning experience—involvement.

Spelling can be taught *naturally* by the teacher. If the child does not know how to spell the word, the first letter and a line can serve as a "word." The teacher can later spell the word for the child or assist him in deciding how to encode the sounds. Helps, such as the charts and dictionary mentioned in the writing activities, will also assist in learning to spell.

Alphabet Charts

The teacher can simplify matters involving spelling if charts are placed around the room in alphabetical order listing the spelling of words children ask most frequently. The following are a few examples of such words:

a	*b*	*c*	*d*	*e*	*f*	*g*
as	big	can	do	every	for	give
always	because		don't			
and						

The Alphabet and Its Place in Skills Development

The alphabet can be used in a variety of ways. As we described in the guidelines, when the teacher writes the child's words, she verbally identifies the names of letters she prints unless the child knows them. As the teacher does so, the child says the word letter by letter. He then moves into an independent level of letter identification because of the intrinsic nature of the motivation. At this point, letter sounds are taught—not in isolation, nor in nonsense syllables—but in the context of the child's communication.

The first thing a teacher must do to help the student is see that the alphabet is at eye level. The familiar black cards placed at the top of the chalkboard will not do; although these cards could be brought down from the top of the chalkboard, it is better to have a complete set of large cards of a different type. Each letter should have a picture of an object that begins with that letter.

Another lifesaver for the teacher is the individual dictionary. Individual dictionaries can be constructed by stapling twenty-six sheets of paper together, with the letters of the alphabet at the top of each page. The child simply turns to the page that has the beginning sound of the word he needs. He then takes the dictionary to the teacher, tells her the word he wants, and she records it for him. The pages will look much like the letter charts on the wall.

Because we feel the alphabet is so important, we urge the reader to examine the sample alphabet set that we have inserted on the preceeding pages (figure 15). These alphabet cards are part of the material teachers weave together as they begin to teach writing in the way we describe.

The sequence of instructional events can now be seen. We go into detail in the next chapter, but let us state here that:

1. The child says the key word.
2. The teacher prints it on a study card.
3. The pupil calls out each letter as it is printed.
4. When the teacher realizes that the given word begins with a labial sound, she proceeds to reinforce that sound so that the child will be less likely to need to ask how to start any word that begins with it.
5. Each letter identified is referred to in some way on the posted set of alphabet cards within eye level of the children.
6. The child takes his word and "does something" with it.

FIGURE 15

57

C c

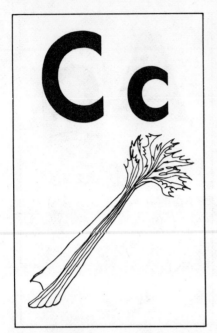

D d

E e

E e

Figure 15, continued

F f

G g

G g

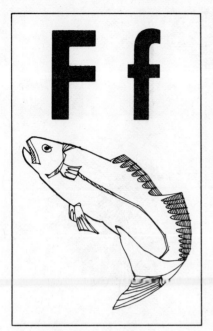

H h

FIGURE 15, continued

59

I i

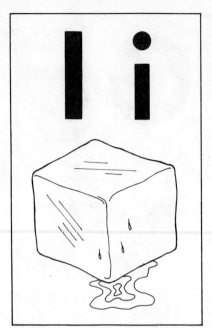

I i

J j

K k

FIGURE 15, continued

60

L l

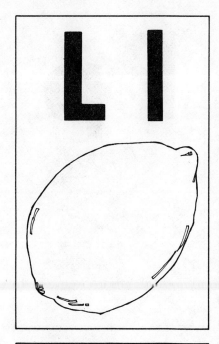

M m

N n

O o

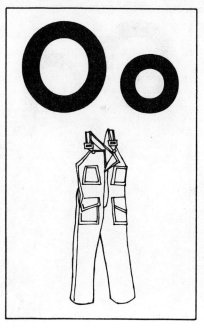

Oo

Pp

Qq

Rr

Figure 15, continued

62

S s

T t

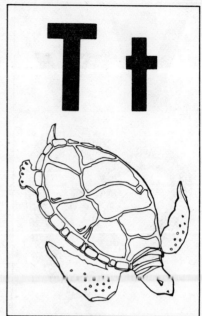

U u

U u

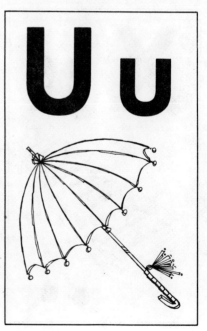

FIGURE 15, continued

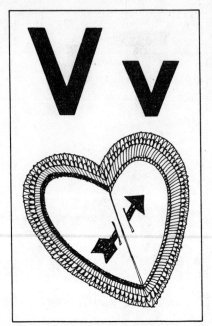

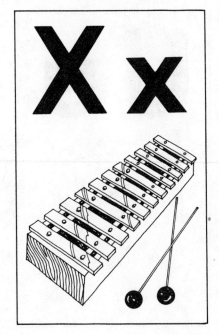

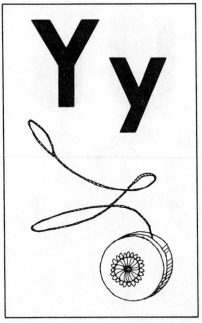

FIGURE 15, continued

64

Z z

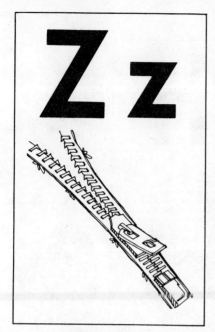

Ch

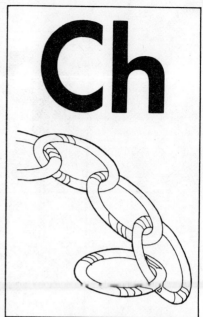

Sh

Th

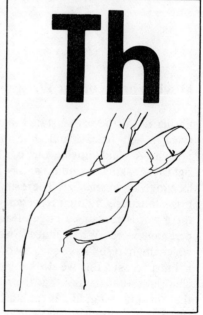

FIGURE 15, continued

FIGURE 15, continued

Moving into Longer Written Material

Earlier in this book, we stated that key vocabulary is an early initiating stage to help teacher and child move into the language experience approach. A child moving out of the "giant-word syndrome" develops significant skills in reading and writing through the thought units we are labeling *key vocabulary.* These single, one-look words that can be learned instantaneously by sight represent a hundred or more words, but each of these words contains a large meaning which is pinned down to a single pregnant word. What, indeed, would be the extent of recorded words which might result from such a word as *ghost, monster, boo,* or *Daddy*? It is hard to say. But we do know that the power of these words helps children to understand that their heads are full of ideas. And we know that this understanding is the start of literacy. Each word, to again borrow Sylvia Ashton-Warner's term, is a *caption* of a large-thought unit.

But time passes as children work together in groups and classes; the teacher cannot forever remain at the one-word-per-child level of communication. Larger amounts of writing must be obtained from the children.

FIGURE 16
Child and teacher edit together

At first, this is usually done by taking dictation from a group or even the total class. Sometimes these stories are genuine experiences common to every person present; sometimes they are vicarious experiences for most of the class, a fact which does not necessarily decrease their value. The term "experience stories" can be applied to any written or dictated material that a teacher transcribes for her class. Although it is not necessarily an accurate term, it does have value, since most teachers know that it refers to original material dictated by students (usually in a total-class situation) and written down by the teacher on large sheets of chart paper. As the children progress, though, there is a parallel progression from single-sight words to much longer written material.

Correction of Writing

In working with longer stories, teachers find it hard to resist correcting the errors they find in their pupils' writing. But they must resist this temptation. It does not help to mark up a paper with the well-known red pencil, which may do damage to the child's drive to write. Children may be so discouraged by seeing such corrections that they will not feel like trying hard to spell words they do not know. On the other hand, children will use such words as "gigantic," "enormous," "tremendous," and "magnificent" instead of "big" and "large," if they are not threatened with the fear of misspelling words. If a child needs help, he should be assured that his teacher will work with him, side by side.

Please, teachers, then, no red pencils! No happy or sad faces, no stars, etc.! Nothing must get in the way of a child's wanting to put ideas down on paper.

Yet children must learn the skills of spelling, punctuation, grammar, and all of the other matters of mechanics that relate to writing. What to do? Mauree Applegate said it best when she stated, "Change a child's spelling by helping him to help himself, not from blood left by the red marking pencil."[9] If a child is not penalized, his writing vocabulary will come closer to his speaking vocabulary. That is, he will communicate much more vividly, more fluently, and with less anxiety and upset to himself and others. In short, he will acquire the love of writing. Rigid correction of mechanics can kill that urge.

FIGURE 17
Writing a story about a picture

---

[9]Mauree Applegate, *Easy in English* (Evanston, Illinois: Row, Peterson and Co., 1962), p. 474.

Phonics Begins with Initial Labial Sounds

Labial sounds are those formed by the lips, such as *b, p, f, m,* and *v.* Since these are the sounds a child can "feel," they are the easiest ones for most children to learn. As soon as the teacher finds a word containing such a sound, she should ask the children for other words with the same initial letter. She can thus begin instruction in phonics. Since she does not want to encourage sound distortion, such as *buh,* she should proceed in a manner something like the following:

> Start to say the word *bear.* Don't say *bear,* just get your mouth ready. Start to say it but don't make any noise. Now look at the alphabet cards. What picture word feels like the one you are ready to say? What other words can you think of that feel like *bear?*

Letter sounds are taught from the assumption that most letters sound like their names or nearly enough like their names to be identifiable. Research indicates that if a child develops the ability to perceive beginning letters first, those same letters in final or medial positions will be easier to acquire.

Labials are easy to start with because they are visible to the eye. For this reason teachers of the deaf begin with labials in teaching lip reading. Letters that are made with the lips can be seen and felt. Soon children catch on to the *idea* of beginning to say a word but not making a sound lest they say some sort of gibberish, such as *buh* or *guh.* Once children get the idea of fixing their mouths to begin to say a word, they can be led on to the more difficult tasks of learning to begin words with dentals (i.e., *d* and *t*), sibilants (i.e., *s, sh,* and *z*), gutterals (i.e., *r, l,* and hard *g*), and other sounds.

Write What You Hear

A child should be encouraged to write only the part of the word he knows and to put a line for the rest of the word until the teacher can help find the other letters. At first, most children should be helped to put only the beginning sound, thus teaching left to right directionality.

In the beginning writing stages, a child may write "M_____ cat r_____ up a t_____." At a later stage of writing, the same sentence may read: "My cat r__n up a tr__." The final stage would be, of course, one in which all or most of the letters of each word are included: "My cat ran up a tree."

Rhea Paul,[10] in pursuing the suggestions of Charles Read,[11] observed four stages of spelling that merit far more extensive exploration.

1. Writing the first letter or phoneme of each word or syllable.
2. Adding a final phoneme of the word or syllable, while still omitting short vowel sounds.
3. Giving equal value when writing to all sounds formed *similarly in the mouth,* even if they represent different letters.
4. Spelling exhibits movement more closely resembling standard forms.

In addition, Carol Chomsky[12] has published similar observations that are in general agreement of the strategies espoused in this text.

Final Sounds

The next stage of development is that of final sounds. The teacher has already encouraged the child to identify the sound he hears first. Now, the teacher asks the child to identify the sound he hears last, and to put a line in the middle to indicate that part of the word is missing. For instance, if a child writes *tre* for *tree,* the perfect opportunity to teach the double *e* has presented itself.

Sounds in Medial Position

The final stage is learning the medial sounds. As difficulty arises, the rules that apply to this stage can be taught. An example of a word that has a middle not easily heard is *dark.* At first, a child might write "d__k." A teacher noting this would teach him immediately that *ar* says *are* (see the "Sequence of Phonics"). She would then ask the child to recognize an *ar*-sound in other words, such as *sharp, market, farm, alarm.* There is no guarantee that the child will immediately know this sound when he meets it in a new situation, but the chances are good that he will learn the phoneme more easily when he next needs it. In short, the need to know motivates the acquisition of mechanical skills. The child who insists, "I

---

[10]Rhea Paul, "Invented Spelling in Kindergarten," *Young Children* 21 (March 1976): 1968. Emphasis added.

[11]Charles Read, "Preschool Children's Knowledge of English Phonology," *Harvard Educational Review* 41 (February 1971): 1–34.

[12]Carol Chomsky, "Beginning Reading through Invented Spelling," *Selected Papers from the 1973 New England Kindergarten Conferences* (Cambridge, Mass.: Lesley College, 1973).

want to do it myself" is operating under the same motivation as the child who says, "I want to write it myself."

It is quite common to find children spelling words *as* they hear them. For example, a child's writing *ouda* for *out of,* *gv* for *give,* *brd* for *bird, desrt* for *desert,* and *dzrt* for *dessert* is to be expected and accepted in these early learning periods. Indeed, the teacher should praise children for phonetic spelling by telling them they were "hearing the word just fine," but that there were some missing letters they had to learn "by heart." Teachers will discover what children need to know by watching for these often hilarious misspellings. It is better for a child to spell a word phonetically, albeit incorrectly, than not to spell it at all.

Classroom Management in Teaching Analytical Skills

Once independent writing is under way there are means of assessing skill needs by analyzing the uncorrected papers. As we have stated, we feel there is no reason to correct papers because children do want to write and do not purposely make mistakes. A writing program that has purpose and function can yield high satisfaction when teachers show children how they can write better. For example, suppose a class of twenty-five or thirty children has written some letters or stories. The teacher has scanned the papers and found the outstanding errors. Of course, there may be many more errors than these, but the teacher has chosen to concentrate for the time being on the ones selected. The reader might feel that the teacher should correct *all* the errors, but this is a bit silly as there may be too many to teach anyway. We believe it is better to concentrate on the errors that are the easiest to eradicate, the most glaring, or the major errors of an individual pupil.

Put another way, the teacher learns to skim a given set of papers with a sharp eye for one or two errors that are most easily corrected in a group situation. Perhaps once or twice a month (more often if needed), the teacher chooses to look for certain types of mistakes—punctuation, spelling, usage, tense, or something else.

The teacher then groups the papers according to the type of mistakes children have made and lists the groups in a notebook or on the chalkboard for scheduling during the class day. These groups can be called and instructed, and the errors of these students can be eliminated. Note that only the students who made errors are being taught; they have demonstrated the need for direct teaching. Those who do not need such remediation go about their other academic business.

Here are the sentences that the teacher noticed in one set of original (not necessarily creative, but original) writing.

Anna	I do my job yesterday.
Kenneth	I want to tun the page.
Tom	The children are interesting in the fire engine.
Philip	I saw a gil in a long dress.
Nancy	You bont like me.
Rikki	The bid flew away.
Frank	Your hair is culy.
Sione	The dirb sang in the tree top.
Larry	The danana is green.
Susan	Last Sunday I eat popcorn.
Pata	I cry last night.
Tele	The sky is dlue.

The teacher decided to group the children according to three errors: Past tense group, *D* and *B* reversal group, and Vowel-affected-by-*r* group. This is the way the names were listed to be called for instruction: first the error was written, then a slash mark, and the correction. The list was handy for reference.

Past tense group		*D and B reversal group*	
Anna	do/did	*Nancy*	bont/dont
Tom	interesting/interested	*Sione*	dirb/bird
Susan	eat/ate	*Larry*	danana/banana
Pata	cry/cried	*Tele*	dlue/blue

Vowel-affected-by-r group	
Kenneth	tun/turn
Philip	gil/girl
Rikki	bid/bird
Frank	culy/curly

This activity can be carried out once a week in the beginning of the school year. But if the groups are taught effectively—and this might be the only time workbook exercises would have any relevance to learning—as time passed, corrections would need to be done mainly on a one-to-one basis, and rarely in a group.

What follows is a sample list of errors gleaned from children's writing. Properly grouped, these errors provide clues and what is, in essence, a completed lesson plan for the teacher. In front of the slash mark is what the child wrote; after the slash, what the child should have written.

Tavini	their/there	Senga	spuky/spooky
Jason	you'r/you're		seletons/skeletons
Mary	blud/blood	Bella	bon't/don't
Debby	ansrd/answered		cant/want
			sar/scare
Albert	like/light	Rudy	win/when
	mack/match		i/I
	mack/mask		in stand/instead
Sono	are/our	Nat	higt/high
	no/know	Olive	becaeus/because
George	to/two		put/but
Vince	nigth/night	Jan	i/I
Dave	becas/because	Queenie	insentit/isn't it
	wach/watch	Rosa	too/to
	wen/when		
Jim	becos/because	Helga	wint/went
	bud/blood		houes/houses
	gust/just	Ted	pay/play
	deth/death		qv/give
	tun/turn		

All of the following groups could be set up from this list.

Homonyms			*Blends*	
Tavini	their/there		Dave	wen/when
Rosa	too/to		Senga	seleton/skeleton
George	to/two		Jim	bud/blood
Sono	are/our		Rudy	win/when
	no/know		Bella	sare/scare
			Ted	pay/play

Contractions			*Beginnings of words*	
Jason	you'r/you're		Jim	gust/just
Queenie	isentit/isn't		Bella	bont/don't
				cant/want
			Olive	put/but

Endings of words		Vowel diphthongs	
Albert	like/light	Mary	blud/blood
	mack/match	Dave	becas/because
	mack/mask	Senga	spuky/spooky
Vince	nigth/night	Jim	bud/blood
Nat	higt/high		becos/because
	ghot/ghost		
Helga	houes/houses		

These groups can be called together and taught from selected words on the lists we present under the Sequence of Phonics, using the children's writing to offer clues.

In the beginning, this kind of evaluation may be necessary once a week, but soon twice a month will be ample unless something seems to be wrong. Eventually, it will not need to be done on an entire-class basis at all, and problems of individual children can be handled individually.

A check sheet (figure 18) is designed for the use of a teacher to keep a record of teaching in two ways. It may be used with individual children, in which case a copy should be duplicated and placed in the teacher's notebook. Then, as each task has been demonstrably mastered— probably by examining some writing once or twice a month, or oftener if necessary—it can be checked off. The check sheet also can be modified into a class chart to record what has been taught and when. Samples of dates are included to illustrate how it would go.

Creative Writing

Creative writing is that portion of the school program in which the children are free to use their imaginations. This is the time when children can let out those bottled-up feelings they can't seem to tell anyone about, when they reveal how they feel and how they think, when they are not penalized for making up some fantastic story that adults wouldn't believe anyway—when children are thinking as children.[13]

Sometimes young children cannot distinguish between writing that has a practical element and that which is more personal and emotional. Alvina Burrows suggests that the difference between these elements is that the latter is intensely private, whereas the former is intended for other peo-

---

[13]For an excellent anthology of children's creative writing, see Kenneth Koch, *Wishes, Lies, and Dreams* (New York: Vintage Books, 1970).

CHECK SHEET FOR WRITING

+	−	?
O.K.	Help!	Not sure

Name *John Smith*

Dates of Accomplishment

Items										
I. Punctuation										
Periods & capitals	3/6+									
Quotation Marks	3/10−	3/14−	3/21−	3/23+						
Question Marks	1/6−	1/12+								
Other (use symbol) as : ! , : , etc.	,3/11 ?	3/14+								
II. Handwriting										
Tall & short letter differential	2/4−	2/9−	2/14−	3/1−	3/10+					
Tail letters	2/7−	2/9+								
Hump letters	2/8−	2/9?	2/14?	2/21+						
Pointed letters	2/8−	2/9−	2/15+							
Manuscript to cursive	2/14+									

FIGURE 18

ple's eyes.[14] Inasmuch as this text is addressed more to teachers of younger children than to teachers of those in the middle-childhood years, we might lump all writing into the same category, because younger children will write what they want to. If they are helped, they will share their writings and will be intensely possessive of what they have written. In short, they will combine practical and personal writing in such a way that they are not sure which is which. It really doesn't matter. All that does matter is that the incentive to write is preserved and not spoiled by too rigid a teacher.

With these thoughts in mind, let us describe many activities that children can do on their own. We begin with suggestions for working in a classroom organized for the more personal, intimate kind of writing

---

[14]Alvina Burrows, *They All Want to Write,* 3rd ed. (New York: Holt, Rinehart and Winston, 1965).

FIGURE 19
Thinking before she writes

Classroom Management for Creative Writing. In order for creative writing to transpire in a classroom, a teacher needs to set the stage. The following hints will help in this task:

1. She should create as relaxed an atmosphere as possible in the class-room—one that is free from disturbing noises and commotion.
2. She should have plenty of paper and sharpened pencils on hand. A new ream of paper will do quite nicely.
3. She can begin to set the mood for writing by playing some music, presenting some pictures, or reading some creative stories written by other children. The child need not be limited in his thinking but does need to be free to develop an idea. The stimuli must be multiple.
4. Once the children have started writing, the teacher remains as silent as possible. If she needs to say something, she says it in a very soft tone of voice.
5. If there are children who seem to be having difficulty in coming up with an idea to write about, the teacher walks quietly over to the child and tries to help him develop an idea by asking such questions as: "What do you feel like writing about?" "What kind of a mood are you in—happy, funny?"

6. All children should have an opportunity to finish writing their stories. Should someone finish ahead of the class, that child must find something quiet to do while the others are busy writing.

7. At the end of the writing period, some of the children might like to read their stories to the class, although this should not be insisted upon. There are those shy children who want to read although they will not volunteer; in this instance, some prodding by the teacher might help. For example, she can ask the child if he would want her to read his story. By beginning to read that story, then gradually handing it over to the child to finish reading, the teacher can elicit an effort from a shy child.

Because of its emotional impact, creative writing cannot be done very often during the week; one day, perhaps Friday afternoon, will do. During the week, children can be doing other kinds of writing activities.

Letter Writing

Another powerful and practical incentive for a child to write is the knowledge that an adult he knows wants a letter from him. The child may be encouraged by being allowed to write a letter to a "real" person anywhere in the world, saying whatever he wants to say, and being assured that the letter will be mailed.

Each pupil must feel that this letter will be a private communication. He can ask for help, but the teacher will help with spelling and punctuation only if asked.

There is no need for a prelesson in letter writing. The form of the letter will come as it is needed. The child first writes his letter on scrap paper and, if he desires, the teacher can check for spelling and punctuation marks. Once the child is sure that he has written all he wants, he takes a sheet of clean paper and rewrites his letter as neatly as possible. The final copy is inserted into an envelope, sealed and stamped by the child, and addressed with the aid of the teacher. After every child who is sending a letter has his envelope ready, the children gather together and walk to the mailbox with the teacher to mail their letters. The activity becomes more meaningful when the child carries out every step himself.

Letter writing teaches more in the curriculum area of language arts than almost any other activity, yet it is among the least expensive, requiring only paper, pen, an envelope, and a stamp.

The Use of Photographs

If the teacher displays photographs in a place where everyone can see them, she can then ask if one child or a group, with the help of the teacher, would like to write a story about one of the pictures. The children or individual child sit next to the teacher and to the picture that is being written about. If the child cannot write, the teacher takes on the role of stenographer and writes what the child says. Once the story is written, the child is asked to read it. If corrections are needed, they can be made either during dictation or during reading. The point is to edit with the child, in order for the child to see what constitutes errors and what must be done about them if his writing skills are to improve.

The teacher might be able to type the stories; typed stories take on more meaning for their authors because they see their words printed in the same way that words in a book are printed. The completed stories and photographs can then be taped onto drawing paper and made into a booklet, or mounted in a dime-store photo album.

The steps described above can also be used with magazine pictures, newspaper articles, etc. Any picture or illustration can provoke a story.

Story Writing Ideas

1. Make each child's own writing pad or journal. Individual snapshots of the children can be taken and mounted on separate sheets of loose-leaf paper or on the first page of a writing tablet. On the front cover of loose-leaf pad or tablet, the teacher can write something personal—"My Story Pad," "All My Stories"—to let the child know that this is his possession.
2. Plenty of paper for children's own books should be provided. Children can put pages together and draw and write their own picture story book.

Using Children's Writings

Once a child has completed writing a story or making a book, he doesn't have to take it home where it can be forgotten. Rather, it can become a library book to read during free moments, share with other classes, and refer to for help with spelling.

Professional literature has been blessed with an exceptional group of texts to help teachers move in the same direction advocated here. We feel special mention should be made of John Stewig's *Read to Write,* Richard Lewis' *Miracles* and *Journeys,* and R. Van Allen's text, *Language Experiences in Communication,* as well as the work of Kenneth Koch and the classics by Mauree Applegate and Alvina Burrows already mentioned. Alan Bullock's *Language for Life* covers the gamut from kindergarten through high school, and most clearly explains its thesis in chapter eleven.[15]

Activities for Experience Stories

1. Real objects can be presented to stimulate discussion. For example, the children might pretend they are describing the object to a friend on the telephone or to someone who is blind. The object should be something of interest, such as a live animal, a toy, a piece of machinery. The children should be encouraged to find different ways to say the same thing in describing the object. All answers are acceptable; talk is to be encouraged, not discouraged.

2. Pictures might be placed in the chalk tray. Children can then move to a picture they want to talk about, and small discussion groups may develop.

3. A picture or transparency might be displayed for the children to see. They are then asked, "What would you like to ask about this picture?" or, "What would you like to know about the picture you see?" The children will respond to questions when this technique is used.

4. The morning "Newstime" or "Show and Tell" can be conducted by the children themselves. They select a different chairperson each week who is responsible for the discussion. The teacher records caption words during "Newstime." These can be written up as an experience story or typed as a newspaper. One teacher found that if she allowed her children to play with clay during "Newstime," the period went very smoothly. The use of clay allowed the children to release pent-up emotions in a constructive way.

---

[15]Stewig, *Read to Write* (New York: Hawthorne, 1975); Lewis, *Miracles: Poems by Children of the English-Speaking World* (New York: Simon & Schuster, 1966); idem, *Journeys: Prose by Children of the English-Speaking World* (New York: Simon & Schuster, 1969); Van Allen, *Language Experience in Communication* (Boston: Houghton Mifflin, 1976); Koch, *Wishes, Lies, and Dreams*; Applegate, *Easy in English*; Burrows, *They All Want to Write*; Bullock, *Language for Life.*

5. After toys have been arranged on a shelf, each child might describe to the teacher the toy he wants to play with. He should not be allowed to name it or point to it. This same idea may be used for any type of object, such as a tray of cookies, a bowl of candy, a book.

6. One of the surest ways of getting a child to talk is through the use of a self-photograph, snapped when the class is involved in some activity in or out of the classroom. If a Polaroid is available, the child can see himself in a matter of seconds. The children will then gather around close enough for everyone to have a clear view of the picture. The teacher can start the conversation by asking the simple question, "What is happening in this picture?" and the children will take care of the rest. All the teacher does is try to capture the caption words from the conversation.

7. The saying that "a picture speaks a thousand words" is certainly proven by a child telling what he sees in a picture. When a child looks at a picture—whether in a magazine, newspaper, or on a billboard—he sees things that no one has to tell him about, but it is up to the teacher to draw out those words from the child that express his feelings.

8. The children themselves can be allowed to find their own sentence on the experience chart and cut it out. Each child can then mount his sentence on a large sheet of paper and illustrate it. Finally, the illustrated sentences can be placed back in order and bound together to make a book.

9. Experience charts can be kept on a rack so that children can read them whenever they want. After several stories have been collected, they can be placed between two large sheets of cardboard or oaktag to form a large book. The book may be held together with shower curtain rings, clothespins, yarn, or notebook rings. The "big book" can be placed in the library center.

10. A long sheet of butcher paper can be taped on the chalkboard and the children allowed to color a sequence of pictures about a field trip. The children then write their stories under each picture on the chalkboard. After stories have been edited, the children copy them on the paper.

Making an Alphabet Book

1. The child looks through a magazine for different pictures beginning with the various letter sounds of the alphabet.

2. Whenever he finds a picture he likes, he cuts it out and pastes it on a sheet of drawing paper.

3. He then writes the first letter name of the picture somewhere on the drawing paper with a crayon.
4. All of these pages can be made into a booklet.
5. On the front cover, the child writes a title of his own choosing.
6. The child has just made his own alphabet book. This booklet becomes his personal property for him to use whenever needed.
7. This activity can be continued by having the child write the picture names on the paper. However, this step might require the aid of the teacher. The child should only do those pictures of which he is sure.

Other Activities

1. Charts can be hung on the walls with a letter of the alphabet written on top of each. As words are asked by the children, the teacher alphabetically records those words which are asked most frequently.
2. Dictionaries can be made using words other than nouns that are commonly found in basal readers or elementary dictionaries. As a child needs a word, he finds the section with the correct beginning consonant and looks to see if the word is included. If not, the teacher records the new word that the child need in the dictionary.
3. Children may select their favorite original story to type or have typed and illustrate. Covers are then made, and the "book" is bound for use at the library table or with other classes. Thus, each child truly becomes an author in his own right.

Student Activities for Teachers in a Hurry

1. Writing captions for pictures and paintings.
2. Writing stories to accompany original pictures or paintings.
3. Making charts of words—such as animal words, weather words, color words.
4. Writing notes or letters to classmates. A chart with the letter form can be made and correspondence mailed in a "class mailbox"—another project for the children.
5. Writing stories to make into original books. Stapling pages together and writing titles on covers. Illustrating the stories.
6. Labeling bulletin board displays.

7. Keeping an address file. Each child can write his name, address, telephone number, and birthday there for quick reference.
8. Making and illustrating word books—size words, family words, number words.
9. Having the children write their own drill cards of words that they want to learn.
10. Keeping simple diaries.
11. Writing stories from "idea cards"—"My Family," "My Pet," "My Weekend."
12. Writing poems.
13. Making lists of rhyming words.
14. Writing nonsense poems and stories.
15. Writing invitations, thank-you notes for class activities, field trips, visitors, and programs.
16. Making simple worksheets for other children.

FIGURE 20
Children's original books

Summary

In this chapter on writing, we have pulled together the ideas that demonstrate the interrelationship between reading and writing. The role of mechanics, especially handwriting and spelling, was discussed and reference was made to other portions of the book that deal with related subjects in detail. Particular emphasis was placed on teaching the use of service words in teaching through an experience story. Finally, transferring such skills to fully independent writing at an older age was described.

4

Skill Development
and Phonics

In order to learn to read and write, certain abilities must be present. The question of whether or not all, some, or part of these competencies are taught directly to each student, or are acquired indirectly, determines the way a teacher teaches.

We believe in a strategy of developing situations in which skills and abilities are self-taught to a large degree. This is not to say that nothing in the area of skill development is to be taught directly, nor that everything a child learns must be gained by a kind of intellectual osmosis. For example, learning to make a letter, such as a capital *G* in manuscript or cursive, is a matter that requires direct instruction. "This is the way the pencil goes," says the teacher. "This is the way you hold your pencil."

On the other hand, the recognition of "words in my head" is a matter that results from a situation staged by the teacher, who then must wait until realization dawns on the learner that she can think of different words with elements similar to the one that is a model.

"Phonics" has come to mean that strategy whereby letters in a word are studied as sounds, so that the reader may analyze the word. We are in agreement with Frank Smith when he said:

> Children could not possibly learn to read through the medium of spelling-to-sound correspondence rules which are far too cumbersome and unreliable for anyone ever to be able to use them effectively. But I do not suggest that

85

teachers immediately stop using whatever they call "phonics" in the class-room, especially if the method happens to show results.[1]

Although there is more to skill development than phonics, the monumental error most teachers make in teaching reading is teaching children to analyze words that are imposed upon them from a source unknown to the pupil. When words are analyzed from the bedrock of their origin—the spoken language of the pupil—the strategy of such analysis is markedly different than that used with an unknown, usually adult, source.

The majority of research on word analysis is devoted to observations of the operation with imposed words—those which have not been first spoken or written by the pupil. Once a child knows what she is to read or write, the use of context comes into its full glory. Everything is simpler because the final objective is so apparent.

This chapter includes a discussion on what is usually called "phonics." This section is designed as a back-up of words which might be used when it is necessary to show a pupil new words with component parts similar to those of her own words. Although this section does resemble traditional phonics texts, we do not intend these elements to be taught in isolation. Quite the contrary. If the reader will follow the sequence of instruction laid out in the sections "The Place of Diagnostic Teaching," "Sight Words as Tools," and "Using a Sequence of Phonics," it will be apparent that this text suggests material useful in specific situations, as opposed to teaching daily isolated phonics lessons (e.g., children work on a lesson because it is the next page in their workbooks). This, we believe, is the best of education: fitting the learnings to what the child needs to learn at the time the need arises.

Phonics is only one tool in word analysis and can be misused with words that are not part of the pupil's language. The great strength of the language experience approach is that the first words analyzed are words from the speaking vocabularies of children. When this is the case, all aspects of word attack come into play. As we suggest later, there is a general sequence of the acquisition of word attack skills.

Development of Mechanical Skills

Beginning reading is traditionally based upon a sight-word vocabulary, and key vocabulary is a sight-word method. The difference between this and other methods is that the key words come from the child and have meaning to her as an individual. This power of meaning enables the

[1]Frank Smith, *Psycholinguistics and Reading* (New York: Holt, Rinehart and Winston, 1973), p. 6.

teacher to move naturally from the "wordness" of a sight word into the *structure,* or *analysis,* of words. There is no commercial system that teaches sight words using children's own vocabulary, because one cannot publish that which has not been said.

We feel that the term "sight word," however, is really a misnomer in the way it has traditionally been applied. Dolch insisted that a list of some two hundred words be memorized for instantaneous recognition wherever and whenever met. Teachers drilled and students struggled—without notable success, as we see several decades later. The theory that a certain group of words was so common that they could be memorized by shape, regardless of meaning, flies in the face of how language is learned. Dolch and his contemporaries did not realize that words, in whatever shape, without the context of oral or written expression, are not useful elements in instruction; they did not realize that language is learned from the inside out.

But the words "learning by sight"—learning words by how they look— stuck. And so we have the term "sight words" applied to a vast majority of our vocabulary that, as Roma Gans said many years ago, "glue our language together."[2] These are the words that hold little emotional or dramatic meaning when they stand alone; words, such as *was, the, from, about,* have traditionally been found difficult to teach by most teachers.

Goodman gives a more precise term, "function words," that describes exactly what such words do and establishes such subcategories as *noun marker, verb marker, clause marker, verb particle, intensifier.*[3]

Thus the term "sight words" in the case of Sylvia Ashton-Warner's key vocabulary is true and accurate usage. As we have said, reading words is not a matter of taking meaning from the page, but rather bringing meaning to the page.

As we described in chapter one the words elicited from a child come, as one said so surely, "from my head." These words have meaning at their creation; then, and only then, can they be learned easily by sight, as hundreds of children have consistently proven. It is this instantaneous learning that reveals a unique phenomenon of the practice.

Learning Begins with Large Wholes

To understand the teaching of reading mechanics, the reader must recognize that the direction of all learning goes from large to small. Anyone

---

[2]Roma Gans, *Common Sense in Teaching Reading* (New York: The Bobbs-Merrill Co., Inc., 1963).

[3]Kenneth Goodman, "Analysis of Oral Reading Miscues: Applied Psycholinguistics," in *Psycholinguistics and Reading,* Frank Smith (New York: Holt, Rinehart and Winston, 1973), p. 168.

who has watched a baby develop knows that the arching of her back—a large movement—precedes the use of her hands. Without exception, developmental patterns indicate that all learning begins with large, all-encompassing *wholes*.

From these wholes, perceived in outline form, the gestalt patterns break down into smaller parts. For example, if you, the reader, are a driver of a car, you probably have had the experience of losing your car in a large parking lot. You look and look. Sooner or later, you see a familiar bumper, front end, or some other part of your car. The point is that even if you cannot see *all* of your car, you know, without question, that *it is your car*. How can this be so, unless recognition of wholes takes place before parts? If this were not the pattern, you would have to go and look at the whole car in order to see if it were yours.

Thus, learning to read can be expressed as the following sequence.

1. Large wholes
2. Outside form or shape (front, back)
3. To middles
4. To wholes again

The Place of Diagnostic Teaching

Granted that this progression is accurate, we must insist that diagnostic teaching cannot be done with beginning readers. We feel that the diagnostic approach for beginning reading is wrong because it assumes that something, presumably a problem, needs to be diagnosed. Because diagnostic teaching is based on the idea that something is wrong or missing, such teaching is irrelevant for the learner who has no problems. If you teach *in case* something *may be needed,* you sacrifice relevancy; relevancy can *only* come from meaning and not from instruction in skills that *supposedly* are needed.

Let us argue our point of view further. Diagnosis implies illness, error, or imperfection; it must be, then, negative in nature. It is intended to fix something that has already happened and already gone wrong; therefore, it must come after failure has occurred. In teaching beginning reading, failure has not occurred because *nothing* has occurred. Because the existence of diagnostic teaching is an admission of past failure, it cannot be used to begin reading instruction. The purpose of this text is to get children started off right; thus, diagnostic teaching will not be needed.

But there can be what some might call an informal diagnostic procedure in teaching beginning reading. Perhaps the term "diagnosis" is semantically incorrect. A teacher must be able to observe general development so that he can determine, for example, the part of a word the child can see and the part she cannot see. From this standpoint, teachers are certainly diagnosing an ability to decode. The reason for a child's success or failure to decode a word can be better determined by observing the child's writing.

All of this is not to say that children are unable to learn a teacher-motivated word that comes from a published list. They do learn; but our experience has shown their learning to be arduous and without zest.

With all of this in mind, where does the teacher begin? In what sequence do reading skills develop? How can these skills be developed by a teacher? What can be observed about progressions? These are some of the questions that will be answered in this chapter.

Sight Words as Tools

Key vocabulary words are learned by sight or shape. The intrinsic value of this fact for each child is high indeed. All teachers who have been involved in teaching with sight words have been struck by the possessiveness all children display about their words. It is always difficult to get children to give up the words they have but do not know. It is a curious phenomenon, but one that has been consistently observed.

Mechanical skills can be taught more easily with the "key vocabulary" type of sight word than with the traditional list of words *presented* to children from basal texts. Traditionally, children are taught words in order to read. Under the philosophy and practice described in these pages, children *read in order to learn words*. These viewpoints are diametrically opposed.

When a child gives her key word to the teacher, it can be said that the word is already *encoded* in her thinking; she needs only to learn to *decode* it for later use in a different situation. Decoding is essentially a form of word analysis requiring analytical skill. Therefore, decoding implies a letter-by-letter, phoneme-by-phoneme approach. To see a word as a whole is reading; to see a word as a whole is the skill of recognizing words by sight or by shape. How, then, can the letter-by-letter decoding operation take place as a beginning act of reading? *Total* word perception is the function of using "key words"—sight words—as tools.

The Whole Word Breaks Down.   Teachers using key vocabulary have discovered that the child's key words are recognized instantaneously. Thus, sight words are first seen as whole words; if not, they are thrown away. These teachers have found that a child's sight vocabulary is not as easily developed when the words carry little emotional connotation for her. The greater the emotional impact, the sooner the whole word becomes a part of the child's sight vocabulary. Once such words are recorded, they can be used as a means of recognizing other words that have the same beginning sounds or rhyming sounds. Eventually, the whole word shape will break down, and the child will see and hear the beginning and ending of a word. The middle of a word will be seen and heard last, as most second-grade teachers know.

Words Beginning with Labials

As we have said frequently, the "conversation has to be got." However, out of the many words in this conversation, either when the class is sitting as a whole or when a child is dictating a word or story to the teacher, there will sooner or later come a word that begins with a labial. In chapter three, we have gone into detail on procedures to follow with initial labials; it is from this beginning that the alphabet becomes rational and relevant to the child. Contrary to much educational thinking in recent years, the alphabet is an extremely important part of early instruction. Let us digress here to describe how it fits into our patterns of teaching, and pick up how the teaching of words with initial labials is a precursor to the teaching of phonics.

Alphabet Cards

As we noted in chapter one, alphabet cards should be displayed in the classroom at the children's eye level so that they can refer easily to them. The cards should be clearly visible from across the room.

There should be thirty-three alphabet cards displayed instead of the usual twenty-six. These cards should include all long and short sounds of vowels, the hard and soft sounds of *c* and *g*, and separate cards for *sh, ch, th,* and *ph*. The letters, with both the capital and lower case displayed, and a picture or three-dimensional object having the corresponding initial sound, should be placed on the card. The illustration should fill up most of the space on the card, as shown in figure 21.

Apart from the teacher, these alphabet cards are perhaps the most important resource a child can have. The children should be taught to hunt through the alphabet until they find the first letter of a word they want to spell. Once this first letter is found, the child can ask another child or adult for the rest of the word. If she cannot find the beginning of the

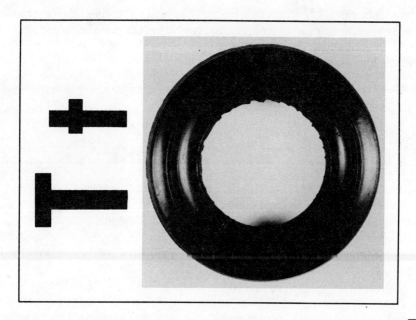

FIGURE 21

word, she can ask for the whole word. Thus, when a teacher sees what has been written, he can immediately assess whether the child has a problem with the beginning, the end, or the middle of the word. Examples of other words and suggested pictures follow.

A	Angel	Apple
B	Ball	
C	Cat	Celery
D	Dish	
E	Eagle	Eggs
F	Feather	
G	Goat	Giraffe
H	House	
I	Ice	Igloo
J	Jam	
K	Kite	
L	Lemon	
M	Moon	
N	Nest	
O	Oatmeal	Octopus
P	Pail	
Q	Queen	
R	Rabbit	
S	Soap	
T	Tomato	
U	U.S.A.	Umbrella
V	Violin	
W	Window	
X	Xylophone	X-Ray
Y	Yo-yo	
Z	Zipper	

Using a Sequence of Phonics

With the alphabet ready and classroom management problems analyzed, let us turn to a discussion of a simple progression of phonics by which children learn to analyze words. In this book, we call the section on pages 95 and 96 the "Sequence of Phonics." It is designed as a quick reference to help teachers see what rules can be taught from the words of a child's language.

This list of rough progressions in the "Sequence of Phonics" can be found in many references dealing with the teaching of phonics. However, we believe that our suggestions regarding its *use* have no parallel anywhere. We insist that these words are usable only when the teacher has found *clues* through the examination and observation of the child's own written language. Because words from teachers' texts are actually abstractions in and of themselves, they are basically irrelevant and meaningless for any given child. Therefore, if we are to suggest that these words be taught by *themselves,* we have fallen into the age-old trap of teaching children without a base of meaning. On the other hand, teaching can proceed from such lists when clues have been found in advance. If the base of meaning is there, it makes both the teaching and the learning simpler, easier, and more understandable. One good way to use this phonics list is to see if a child does or does not know or hear the initial sounds in words. The clue might be that the child cannot hear a blend; for example, if she spells *play* without the *l* (i.e., *pay*), then the teacher can look in the Sequence under "Blends in the Beginnings of Words," and practice with the child hearing such beginning sounds.

In another example, if a teacher, as he works with a child, sees that the child can spell the beginning and the end of a word but is using a line to indicate that she does not hear the middle, then the teacher has the clue to teach vowel sounds. These might be long vowels, such as *meat* or *boat,* or they might be short vowels, such as *back* or *pill.* The might even be vowels affected by *r,* such as *bird, hurt,* or *firm.*

One final example might be a child who wants to spell "family" in her writing. The teacher recognizes that the skill of spelling a multisyllable word depends upon the separation of the word into syllables by saying it, clapping or tapping at each syllable, and listening to the sounds in the first, or accented, syllable (in this case *fam*) and spelling it. Thus, the teacher turns to the section "Compound Words" or to "Multisyllable Words."

These are three illustrations of how these lists, which are basically abstract and irrelevant, can be given a direct, meaningful relationship to the relevant language of any child. *To repeat, once a child has some talk that she wants to write down, and in so doing reveals certain problems, these problems produce the clues by which the teacher can teach her the elements missing from her ability to attack words.*

Two Basic Rules for Phonics

There are two rules that are absolutely necessary for the use of these lists.

1. The child's own words dictate which samples from the lists are selected, because selection must be based upon the needs revealed in the child's writing or reading. Thus, these lists become intrinsic rather than extrinsic or imposed.
2. Gibberish (nonsense syllables or nonwords) must be avoided as much as possible.

We have explained the first rule with our previously cited examples. Let us discuss the second.

Gibberish is that kind of language that has no meaning in and of itself. The sound of *b* is often heard as *buh.* We believe that the use of initial labials as described earlier is clearly a successful way to avoid any confusion of letter name and letter sound. Gibberish in the initial position is avoided by the use of the names of the letters in the alphabet that sound enough like their names to be recognizable. For example, once a child hears that *feather* begins with the letter *f,* then she can use the technique of substitution to make another word that *begins* like *feather* but rhymes with *round.* She can thus master the word *found* without resorting to the method of *fuh—ound.*

When working with the end of a word, teachers too often tend to describe a word pattern or family by such nonwords as the *ook, ick,* or *ight* words. Using the same procedures as described above, the teacher can help a child to put fronts and backs of words together to find the desired word.

Having described these basic introductory rules, let us present the progression of learning phonics that we have been discussing. These are word attack skills. While we do not feel that every child needs to be taught every rule or discover every commonality, teachers should be aware that this listing roughly follows a developmental pattern of learning. As we said earlier, it is necessary that the child:

1. Sees and hears *wholes* first.
2. Then recognizes *ends* of words—fronts and backs.
3. Last, struggles to gain power over the *middles* of words.

Certainly, some children go through this progression without anyone's being aware that they have. The teacher may be surprised to find a child who is suddenly having middle-of-word problems when he was not aware that the child had mastered the alphabetic principle with naming initial sounds. It may be that children skip around such a listing without an orderly developmental pattern. This does not matter. The important thing is that the teacher can extract from the clues available those necessary samples he requires to help the child discover what she needs.

This brings us to our final step. If our basic teaching tenet is intrinsic, then working from a clue, we must present several samples from our "Sequence" of words and *have the child tell us what she discovers.* The use of discovery is far easier when developed from a base of meaning. We see discovery of abstractions as just that—a meaningless mass of gibberish without recognizable connection to the pupils' need to communicate in writing or to gain knowledge through reading. A puzzle is always harder when you don't know what you're working towards.

We stress that the following phonetic sequence is designed to *save* teacher's time. We are presenting here examples that can be used when a child shows she needs help. But if these words are used before the need for help is demonstrated, the whole base of meaning that provides the child with the context of what she is trying to say or write is nullified. The Sequence of Phonics is a valuable teaching aid in every sense of the word, but its value rests on proper use.

Sequence of Phonics and Explanation

I. *Recognition of Ideas as Written*

   A. Sight Vocabulary

      1. Learning words by their shapes as they appear first, through children's experiences, and then in vicariously oriented material.

II. *Development of Word Analysis Skills*

   A. Beginnings of Words

      1. Applying the alphabet, using names of letters when possible.

      2. Learning to hear, and eventually see consonant blends and digraphs.

   B. Endings of Words (or the rest of the word without initial letters)

      1. Ending sounds of words.

      2. Families of words.

   C. Middles of Words (vowel sounds)

      1. Long vowels as learned in initial, final, and middle positions.

2. Long vowel rules.

   a. *E*-on-the-end rule

   b. Two-vowel rule (sometimes called "vowel digraph")

3. Vowels affected by *R*.

   a. *Ar*-says-*are* rule.

   b. *Er* rules (*er, ir, ur,* and sometimes *or*).

4. Short vowels.

   a. *A* as in *apple, E* as in *Eskimo, I* as in *Indian* or *igloo, O* as in *octopus, U* as in *umbrella.*

5. Vowel diphthongs.

   a. *oi* as in *oil, ou* as in *out, au* as in *haul,* etc.

D. Parts of Words

1. Syllables, prefixes, and suffixes.

2. Small words in bigger words when useful.

I. Recognition of Ideas as Written[4]

I.A. Sight Vocabulary

E.W. Dolch compiled this list of 220 words and claimed that these words make up 50 to 75 percent of all school reading matter. He advocated that they be learned by sight, and did not refer to any practice of first eliciting them from a pupil's own mind. As we have said, the original use of words is the most important part of becoming a literate person. However, teachers do have a need for illustrations; thus, this list can be used as a kind of check sheet for teachers using experience charts. These words can be used to teach initial consonants, short vowels, or any other phoneme. In short, learning them "by sight" is unncecessary.

try	best	ask	down	call	three
found	an	read	write	under	am
grow	always	jump	ate	pick	was
tell	now	fly	so	sit	let
want	these	said	shall	make	will

---

[4]The following word lists are modified after and expanded upon Jeannette Veatch, *Teaching Reading in the Elementary School,* 2nd ed. (New York: John Wiley & Sons, Inc., 1979).

around	full	but	good	at	kind
pretty	carry	please	did	get	yellow
brown	far	soon	that	there	when
better	went	come	his	been	clean
with	run	must	or	them	my
were	one	too	together	I	only
are	keep	not	they	green	play
wish	got	big	saw	seven	know
come	cut	warm	at	she	ton
just	help	where	all	would	show
because	say	four	work	right	both
use	five	think	ran	what	sleep
put	blue	this	how	hurt	your
think	has	he	can	ever	be
here	look	have	me	going	from
about	go	gave	we	give	off
old	well	some	new	two	pull
ride	done	don't	live	for	wash
drink	red	into	of	own	they
thank	sing	its	myself	long	by
first	much	they	yes	cold	do
her	why	and	many	you	eat
little	round	fall	light	to	goes
draw	out	on	funny	those	in
may	after	our	if	find	buy
every	walk	their	once	today	had
no	white	never	which	like	not
very	see	is	as	who	
snail	take	open	him	upon	
us	away	start	laugh	fast	

II. Development of Word Analysis Skills

II.A. Beginnings of Words

The Alphabet Principle. With the exception of *H, W, Y,* hard *G,* and short vowels, all letters sound either like their names (the long vowels) or *enough* like their names to be recognized when heard in a word.

The easiest place to teach any letter sound (phoneme) is in the beginning of a word; the next harder place to teach and/or hear it is at the end of a word; the hardest task of all is to recognize letter sounds in the middles of words. That is why our sequence is so constructed. It is truly in order of perception—visual *and* auditory.

When the alphabet cards are placed at eye level, children can easily match the letters in their early key words to the appropriate letter card. Indeed, each time a child needs to know how to start a word, she can be referred to those cards. She can be helped by acquiring the skill of identifying those phonemes which are letters sounding like their names. And eventually, of course, all must learn by memory those letters that have a sound all of their own. Those few letters that sound like other letters (*c* for *k, g* for *j*) are also subject to memorization.

II.A.1. Applying the Alphabet Principle

Soft c (s sound) Sounds like its Name

cent	cereal	center	central
city	certain	circle	cyclone
circus	cycle	circuit	celery
cement	ceiling	cinder	

Soft g (j sound) Sound like its Name

giraffe	genie	gyroscope	gentle
gypsy	gymnasium	giant	geography
Gene	genius	genuine	George
gerbil	German	gem	general
germ	gelatin	gender	geology

II.A.2. Consonant Blends and Digraphs

Blends

clay	grape	fly	crayon
draw	brown	pray	street
tree	black	plan	stripes
smile	spring	gleam	splash
free			

CH Digraph

children	chop	change	chew
chair	chicken	cheese	Chuck
chase	cherry	chick	child
chime	chance	China	church

SH Digraph

she	shake	shale	sheep
shudder	Shawn	sheet	shirt
short	shoulder	shadow	shall
shell	should	shine	shoot

TH Digraph

think	three	thing	those
the	these	than	third
thick	thumb	this	there
they	their	then	that
throw	thank	thresh	them

PH Digraph

These digraphs are taught as an *f* sound; the letters must be learned by memory.

phonograph	phone	phobia	pheasant
phase	Philco	physical	phantom
Phoenix	Philippines	Philip	Phoebe
phlox	phony	phrase	Philadelphia

II.B.1. Ending Sounds of Words

Vowels

Mexico	three	yoyo	Ohio
oleo	I	day	rodeo
free	radio	agree	frisbee
bray	spree	you	play

Soft c (s sound)

fancy	dance	prince
chance	lance	nice
advice	twice	ace
niece	lace	mice

Soft g (j sound)

bridge	fudge	page
edge	orange	charge
age	cage	change
dungeon	strange	large

Blends

able	cradle	trust
risk	dust	blast
roost	ghost	moist
nest	cable	brisk
table	twist	middle

CH Digraph

each	match	scratch	lunch
much	stitch	teach	witch
such	ditch	watch	inch
catch	patch	which	rich

SH Digraph

wash	Oshkosh	English
wish	blush	thrush
splash	dish	leash
fish	ash	crash

TH Digraph

with	dearth	lathe
earth	breath	strength
teeth	mouth	hearth
bathe	cloth	blacksmith
smooth	scathe	youth

II.B.2. Families of Words

right	raw	going	day	pay
night	paw	hopping	hay	today
slight	awful	trying	playing	Wednesday
frightened	lawn	ring	away	played
midnight	jaw	swing	Friday	ways
bright	hawk	running	staying	yesterday
tight	shawl		always	Monday
mighty	straw	joy	way	maybe
light		boy	pay	lay
fright	bring	enjoy	Saturday	may
	string	toy	Tuesday	Sunday
saw	sing	destroy	gray	gay

stay	rock	low	naughty	went
Thursday	dock	bowl	daughter	sent
unkind	sick	row	haughty	bent
behind	trick	shallow		lent
remind	brick	flow	how	rent
wind	tick	slow	brown	tent
blind	nick	grow	plow	new
find	quick	hollow	down	knew
grind		follow	cow	news
bind	back		now	mew
	sack	would	flower	blew
clock	tack	could	crowd	threw
tock	track	should	frown	chew
sock	pack		owl	flew
knock	quack	caught	shower	screw
		taught		

In the following words, the first letter is silent and must be learned by memory.

wreath	written	wringer	gnash	knew
wrench	wrapper	wrong	gnaw	knob
write	wreck	gnarl	knee	know
wrinkle	wrote	gnat	knife	knot
wrestler	wrap	gnarled	knitting	knowledge
writs	wren	gnome	knock	kneel

II.C.1. Long Vowel

Initial Place in Word[5]

angel	eagle	ice	open	USA
aviator	ear	Idaho	oak	UN
able	eaves	idea	oasis	uniform
Abraham	eat	idle	oatmeal	united
ape	evening	idol	Ohio	union
age	eel	Irene	Oklahoma	unit
April	equals	Irish	old	Utah
	erase	ivy	oleo	use
	Erie		ovary	

[5]In this text, the authors advocate the use of long and short diacritical marks only when the teacher feels the necessity of sound identification through looking at a word (e.g., hăm or slōpe). We feel that no other diacritical marks are necessary although slash marks for syllables (e.g., fam/i/ly) are recommended if the syllables are not separated by a space.

II.C.2. Long Vowel Rules

II.C.2a. E-on-the-End Rule

State that *e* on the end often makes the first vowel long, say the word's name, write the first vowel (*a, e, i, o,* or *u*), or say "*a, e, i, o,* or *u*" depending upon the particular circumstances in which the question of this rule arises. Using the following lists of words, say, "What is the difference between these rows of words?" Several answers can be chosen.

short to long	*short to long*	*short to long*	*short to long*
at-ate	rat-rate	rip-ripe	slid-slide
cut-cute	dim-dime	win-wine	pan-pane
mat-mate	hid-hide	mad-made	spit-spite
tub-tube	rid-ride	pin-pine	strip-stripe
hat-hate	not-note	man-mane	sam-same
can-cane	rob-robe	spin-spine	at-ate
hop-hope			

Then ask, "What is the vowel sound in *at* or *ate?*" Finally, ask, "What makes the difference in sound?" The answer is that *e* on the end of a word often makes the first vowel long.

make	toe	kite	safe	face
cake	hope	ride	face	gave
take	ice	time	ate	race
shake	mice	hide	gate	case
bake	nice	like	made	races
wake	rake	fine	line	place
lake	late	nine	knife	places
sake	date	rice	write	faces
home	name	twice	mile	bite
hole	game	slice	lie	rise
bone	came	wage	wide	wise
wrote	same	age	mine	tie
rope	save	cage	pride	die
				life

Exceptions of one type:

tumble	apple	temple	wriggle	griddle
wobble	sample	gentle	muscle	dimple
trample	resemble	handle	muffle	little
ample	sampler	kindle	battle	bottle
drizzle	assemble	shuffle		

II.C.2b. Middle of Words

The Two-Vowel Rule

This rule is stated in the following way: "When two vowel letters occur together in a word or syllable, the first vowel is usually long and the second usually silent." "When two vowels go out walking, the first one does the talking," is the more commonly known statement.

To teach this rule, say, "What vowel do you hear?" Then say, "What vowels are really in the word?" Finally ask, "How could you say what you notice in these words?"

each	replied	main	faint	wheel
speak	plain	pies	dreamed	raised
goat	seen	saint	speaking	neither
indeed	peak	sweet	eaten	squeak
flies	dream	sea	toast	need
paid	boat	paint	seed	east
ceiling	geese	Easter	street	bait
sleeping	mean	team	laid	seam
bean	sheath	deep	preach	tree
foam	easy	cried	asleep	maid
leave	strain	toad	sheep	sleep
skies	oat	lead	least	seem
train	peanut	peaches	road	peach
lain	reading	seated	wait	beaten
beat	keep	week	heap	breaches
yeast	cries	rain	teeth	leap
cheese	roast	between	coat	green
ties	raise	satisfied	needle	died
coast	afraid	board	meat	lean
maiden	dried	sheik	sheaf	sieze
reached	easier	seat	faint	seat
free	reach	people	seal	float
heat	deeper	knee	feed	pain

II.C.3 Vowels Affected by R

Ar-Says-Are Rule

Say, "What sound do you hear in the middle of the word?" Then ask, "What letters make that sound?"

at-art		*am-arm*	
are	bark	farmer	march
arm	parking	part	marching

far	park	party	large
hard	car	star	charge
card	cart	start	mark
garden	barn	starting	market
dark	farm	started	sharp

Er,-Ir,-Ur,-and-sometimes-Or Rule

Parts of the following words say "r-r-r."

never	father	letter	thirsty	word	hurt
her	ever	flower	stir	worse	turkey
cover	every	cracker	whirl	world	turn
sister	paper	matter	first	worm	burn
river	afternoon	elder	girl	purple	surprise
mother	butter	stir	third	burst	turtle
other	stranger	bird	dirty	church	curl
brother	supper	whirling	circus	furl	fur

II.C.4. Short Vowels

From the following statements, choose the one pertaining to the vowel in question; say it, and then ask, "What letters can you hear in these words?"

"If apple begins with a . . . "
"If Eskimo begins with e . . . "
"If Indian begins with i . . . "
"If octopus begins with o . . . "
"If umbrella begins with u . . . "

This exercise has taught the rule: If there is only one vowel in a word or syllable, that vowel usually has a short sound.

had	rip	tan	son	left	cut
bad	dip	can	sun	it	end
add	slip	ran	fun	hit	bell
mad	ship	man	gun	bit	leg
pad	drip	pan	up	pin	tell
tag	rock	and	cub	tin	hen
am	not	lap	rug	win	den
jam	lot	map	stub	hid	red
ham	doll	till	bet	lid	wet
has	lock	bill	egg	fill	pet
as	box	pick	fell	mill	set
back	hot	kick	well	fit	let
act	fox	miss	men	but	not

dig	cat	kiss	get	nut	toss
big	at	will	ten	hut	top
pig	fat	hill	yes	duck	log
in	sat	him	fed	us	hog
if	fast	six	held	tub	mop
is	an	fix	elm	mud	hop
drop	dot	dog			

II.C.5. Vowel Diphthongs

Say to the students, "What sound do you hear?" Then ask them, "What letters make that sound?"

long double o or oo		short double o or oo	
room	smooth	foot	book
moon	goose	hood	shook
root	cool	good	hook
rooster	fool	wood	cook
shoot	soon	look	took
stool	noon	brook	
caboose	balloon	stood	
school	bloom		

ou as in out		oi as in oil	au as in haul	
out	round	oil	caught	taught
about	flour	join	saucer	because
house	south	boil	haughty	cause
mouse	pound	spoil	daughter	haul
loud	ground	point	auditorium	sauce
aloud	hour	voice		
shout	our			

II.D. Parts of Words

II.D.1. Syllables, Prefixes, and Suffixes

Syllables not Ending in Word Families

In spelling, the child says, "How do you spell _____?" The teacher responds, "Say the word. Clap or tap the word." The number of syllables to be discovered by the pupil is then told by clapping or tapping back to the teacher. Slash marks can be helpful in this situation if the word is left as a whole (*im/prove*).

In reading, the teacher says, "How many vowels do you see?" The child responds, and the teacher "frames" the accented syllable or points to the vowel in it; "What is this vowel sound? What is in front? What is in back?" The teacher then proceeds from left to right until all of the word is worked out in similar fashion.

Syllables can then be worked through sequentially from left to right. Clapping, however, indicates only the accented syllable. Teachers can help children to sound out the accented syllable first, then the unaccented ones will take their usual unimportant place. Accents tend to trigger meaning. Too much emphasis placed on unaccented syllables can kill meaning.

chimney	gasoline	station	nephew
instrument	science	messenger	lovingly
electricity	scientist	special	material
beneath	license	inventory	member
commonest	artificial	inadventure	messenger
material	glycerine	afterward	million
easily	potatoes	arithmetic	neighborhood
picture	probably	factories	loose
returned	usually	diamond	polite
sneezed	quilt	health	protection
collected	minute	suddenly	government
united	beautiful	honest	whether
arranged	pretending	hospital	dynamite
happened	future	ivory	straight
figure	regular	nurse	tornado
improve	perfume	observe	procession
imagination	obtain	persuade	progress
immediate	observation	personal	protest
action	obligation	percolator	provide
vacation	dangerous	only	promote
protection	famous	fairly	arctic
donation	jealous	fully	electric
direction	elastic	joyous	hilly
digestion	mountainous	mighty	magic
exception	murderous	milky	energetic
	nervous	needy	public

Compound Words

The teacher says, "What do you see in this word that you know?"

because	anywhere	blackberry	newspaper
sunset	underground	another	whenever
scarecrow	dreamland	without	dishwasher
something	understand	kingfish	however
afternoon	goldmine	nobody	everything
bullfrog	seasick	sawmill	outside
gunpowder	housework	playground	overhead
sidecar	neighborhood	wagonload	snowstorm
become	rainbow	gunfire	newborn
behind	grandfather	nighttime	headfirst
paintbrush	everything	drugstore	headline
earache	careless	himself	something

Suffixes and Prefixes on Already Identified Root Words

These lists could well supply weekly spelling lists. Saying and then clapping helps here, too, as it does in any multisyllable word.

compound	dispatch	react	uneasy
compare	distress	rearrange	unfold
compass	example	rebuild	agreeable
content	exchange	recall	container
converse	explain	repair	contention
conscience	expensive	remove	conversation
defend	extraordinary	rebound	defensive
delight	extrasensory	report	destructible
depart	inhabit	recapture	expensive
disagree	invent	unless	habitat
disconcert	inland	uncertain	importance
dismal	invest	unfit	invention
dismiss	recommend	unequal	joyous

II.D.2. Small Words in Bigger Words

These words are sometimes taught as families of words.

all	and	patch	dance	corner	told	corn
ball	hand	catch	prince	morning	folder	fork
call	sand	match	since	store	gold	horn
fallen	land	kitchen	pond	forget	sold	wore
hall	stand	ditch	change	floor	cold	horse
tall	grand	itch	send	short	fold	more
wall	handle	witch	friend	north	golden	born
small	under	stand	lend	porch	bold	sort

Small Words are not always Useful

As most experienced teachers know, there are words that have small words in them. Teachers, warned about this fact when a small word bridges over into another syllable (e.g., *th* in *father*), push the child away from the analytical power we are endeavoring to develop. For example, a child who is stuck on the word *father* in the sentence "Daddy means the same as father," might well come up with *fat* and *her* if urged to find a small word. It would be better if the teacher would proceed in this case by saying, "Yes, but *fat* and *her* don't make any sense. Listen: 'Daddy means the same as fat her.' See? It doesn't make sense. Now look at the word again. There is a small word in there, and it sits right in the middle. See it?" (If child doesn't, the teacher can frame *the* to show the child.) This example is one illustration of a reading act. To reverse the process and do the same word as one to be spelled, we would hear:

Child:	How do you spell *father*?
Teacher:	What is the first letter that you hear?
Child:	*F.* (She might even say: "And I hear an *o*")
Teacher:	It does sound like an *o,* but it is an *a.* What else do you hear as you say the word slowly?
Child:	*Th* sound.
Teacher:	Yes, and then on the end is _____?
Child:	R-r-r-r sound. *er*?
Teacher:	Yes. Now, can you write it from your head, or shall I put it on the board for you?

Use of This Sequence

Although the Sequence of Phonics is a true sequence, and its roughly developmental stages conform to many similar sequences in professional literature, it need not be taught in the order presented. Interestingly, the teachers contributing to this book have reported that they did not feel the need to teach phonics in any particular order, once the children were writing copiously enough. In other words, these teachers were in such demand to help their pupils with spelling, they seemed to realize that everything was being covered and that the sequential presentation listed above was not necesary.

Perhaps it would be more accurate to say that the Sequence of Phonics as we present it is probably the way children *learn* to spell, whether or not anyone *teaches* them in that order. Obviously, research is needed on this point, but the fact remains that our project teachers did move away from

Name __Rosie Garcia__   PHONICS CHECK SHEET   [+] [−] [?]
O.K. Help! Not sure

Dates of Accomplishment

ALPHABET:					
Said by rote	1/10 +				
Identified by sight, one-to-one	1/15 −	1/16 −	1/8 ?	1/20 +	
ABILITY TO SPELL *NEW* WORDS FROM:					
Beginning sounds:　　　*ALL*			?	?	+
Labials	1/10 +				
Sibilants	1/12 −	1/13 −	1/16 ?	1/18 +	
Dentals	1/18 −	1/20 −	1/21 −	1/24 ?	1/26 +
Others		?	?	+	
Endings:					
Rhyming	1/20 +				
"Family"	1/22 +				
Substitution from beginnings	1/22 −	1/23 −	1/26 +		
Middles of Words:	−	−	?	?	+
Heard long vowels	1/6 +				
Heard vowels affected by *R*	1/6 −	1/7 −	1/8 ?	1/12 +	
Heard short vowels	1/6 −	1/7 −	1/10 ?	1/15 ?	
Readable, invented, or phonetic spelling	11/20 +				
Completing own words, phonetically spelled with silent letters.	1/30 −	2/2 −	2/6 ?	2/10 ?	2/12 ?

NOTE: Speech checks are not to be taken from words sounded alone in a gibberish fashion, but rather from words spoken in context.

FIGURE 22

sequential teaching. They felt their children were learning so much during their daily writing sessions that it would be an *interruption* of the activity to have a class lesson on any single point. The following story illustrates this point.

A "future teacher" from a high school was working with a first grader who asked how to spell *phone.* She supplied the answer, but soon afterward, the child indignantly strode over to the teacher and said in disgust, "I asked her how to spell *phone* and look how she began it—with a *p.*" The teacher related later how she immediately called the class to the front board and taught the *ph* phoneme *directly.*

As a result of this and other experiences, let us suggest that this sequence is intended for use as a reference. Research probably will eventually establish that children learn to analyze words in a similar order, but, as stated earlier, we now know only that children learn the *outsides* of words before they learn the middle. Since there is no reason to teach the beginning or the ending of words first, as far as visual perception is concerned, and since western civilization is oriented from left-to-right in approaching language, we might just as well reinforce the direction of our culture and teach the fronts of words before the backs.

The following check sheet is intended for the teacher's record keeping as pupils are helped to write independently. A duplicate set should be in the teacher's notebook. Record keeping need not be a daily affair unless the teacher sees a way of building up day by day to the desired ability. *The check sheet is not a lesson plan;* the items are to be seen as results. In a sense they are objectives, but if used as point-by-point teaching *before* any writing takes place, the value of the Sequence and the actual motivation to write will be destroyed. As children start to write from their own minds, they need a way to record words they do not fully know. Thus, as we have said, the teacher helps them write down those letters that they can recognize from hearing the whole word. Eventually, pupils will be able to memorize the silent letters.

Helps on Skills in Outline Form

1. All skills are rational. They must make sense. No skill should be taught merely to kill time.
2. Remember that the alphabet is crucial.
   a. Keep it at eye level.
   b. Teach children to use it independently.
   c. Sight words are tools; they should be used.

3. Help children to write the letters they can recognize from hearing the whole word.

   Example: *lamb*
   a. l_____ (child hears only the beginning)
   b. l____m (child hears beginning and end)
   c. l a m   (child hears the whole word)
   d. lamb   (child memorizes the silent *b*)

4. All word-attack or word-analysis skills can be taught easier and faster with writing.
5. Writing teaches reading.
6. Powerful ideas simplify the teacher's task of helping children.
7. If there is a need to drill, something is wrong.
8. Reading is a *receiving skill* when a child faces a book.
9. Reading is an *expressive skill* when there is need to hold an audience.
10. Teaching punctuation by having children read their own writing aloud is the best carry-over to good oral reading.
11. Correction is rarely needed in writing, but if it is, do it side by side with the pupil in an individual conference.
12. Teacher and children should enjoy sharing everything—stories, library books, demonstrations.

Perspectives on Grouping

Numerous methods of grouping have appeared to bask in the educational limelight for a time and then "fold their tents and move on."[6] Across the nation, teachers have held on to the three-group plan in the primary grades and the two-group plan in the intermediate grades, with the tenacity of bulldogs.

What actually makes the significant difference in grouping is the *purpose* for the group organization. The majority of practices are set up to place children on various ability levels *before anything is taught*. Content material is divided up like slices of bologna to be doled out to slower children (in smaller slices of knowledge or content), medium-ability children (in slightly larger pieces), and able children (in large hunks of material).

---

[6]Nila Banton Smith, *Reading Instruction for Today's Children* (Englewood Cliffs: Prentice-Hall, Inc., 1963), p. 109.

Many children of high ability know they are being penalized for their ability by being forced to do more of what they don't really need to do in the first place. Children who learn rapidly do not need *more* of the same material; they need tasks that have a quality of uniqueness to them. They need qualitatively different learning tasks.

So, too, tasks for the medium- and low-ability children must be assigned on the basis of need, rather than on the basis of quantity.

Individualized reading has been threatening the foundations of ability grouping for years, because it holds the distinction of being the *only* type of program that groups *after* something has been taught. It assigns children to groups on the basis of tasks to be accomplished. It enables members of groups to cross all ability lines; bright, able children can have just as much trouble with certain tasks as do children whose innate ability is far more limited. Reading aloud, for example, is a task which will find children of all ability levels struggling with problems of expression and inflection—even though each may be reading a different book on a different ability level.

The methodology of self-selection, with its insistence upon learning for valid reasons, mitigates against lining up children on the basis of some teacher-determined need in which they have no personal stake. A child who has not realized her need to learn something can only be made to feel ashamed if grouped in this way. She cannot change her inability to grasp abstract knowledge as fast as another child. The literature on ability grouping is critical in its substantiation of the resulting psychological damage to children, but it is even more damning of the failure of grouping to promote efficiency and good learning climates. Ability grouping is almost worthless in terms of condensing children's needs for easier teaching. Joyous, exciting, stimulating learning can hardly come about when children are grouped with their "peers" in struggling through an imposed lesson.

The steady stream of scientific data concerning reading and child development has given us a new outlook and deeper understanding on grouping. We have come to see that the classroom organization must be ever-changing so that the teacher is able to teach children what they need to learn at the time they need to know it. The purpose of the grouping must be clear not only to the teacher, but also to every child who is a member of the group. At times, there will be one group encompassing the entire class. At other times, there may be different groups of two, three, five, nine, or ten children engaged simultaneously in different activities according to their common needs. Groups are ever-changing in size, purpose, and membership.

Grouping

The basis for any grouping should be determined by assessing portions of children's efforts over a short period of time—perhaps a day, or maybe a week. The teacher is the only one who can do this, for he is the only one who can organize, disband, and reorganize groups according to needs.

Because the need for skill development is best detected through the children's writing, a record of the types of errors made should be kept by the teacher. As the ability to write increases, the number of reading and writing skills should also increase. It is the teacher's role to be aware of the elements of skills development—sequential or not—and to offer a number of ways to develop these skills.

Types of Groups

There are several bases for grouping that lend themselves very well to a classroom set up on intrinsic learning practice. Teachers need not choose one basis for grouping to the exclusion of all others; in fact, if the teacher is attentive to children's needs and interests, several types of groups will be active at any one time.

Skill Groups. Skill groups should be set up only when they are needed and should be discontinued when the given skill has been developed. This means that some groups will last only five minutes; others, perhaps a morning; and still others a day or more. Some children will be able to leave the group after only a short amount of instruction; other children will need more.

The need for skills development can be detected from errors made in writing. For example, if several children are incorrectly putting an *s* or *es* ending on their words, then the need for a skill group has developed. By allowing the group to read the stories they have written, a teacher can discuss with them the need for an *s* or *es* ending. For a more detailed description of such grouping the reader might want to refer to Ronald Cramer's article, "Diagnosing Skills by Analyzing Children's Writing."[7]

Interest Groups. Children are as different as they are alike. Just as some are short and some are tall, so, too, some are interested in animals while

---

[7] Ronald L. Cramer, "Diagnosing Skills by Analyzing Children's Writing," *The Reading Teacher* (December, 1976), pp. 276–79.

others are fascinated by machines. The teacher must encourage exploration of these interests if children are to develop to their fullest. In the
beginning, the teacher may have to pull and probe in order to get the children to express their interests. However, as soon as a positive pupil-
teacher relationship is established, children will pour out their ideas in
numerous ways; this is the springboard into interest groups.

FIGURE 23
Writing together

Interests can be expressed through books from home or school,
"things" (animals, toys, pictures) from home, art work, or conversation.
The teacher can then establish interest groups by:

1. Listing on the board a number of topics the children would like to
   talk or write about.
2. Allowing the children to select one topic from several listed. (Not all
   topics need be used, only those of greatest interest.)
3. Breaking down the class into groups to research a topic. Children
   can research the topic by interviewing people, reading books, finding pictures.

4. Discussing and recording the group's findings once research is completed. If one child in each group is the recorder, the others can tell that child what to write. Large chart paper may be used for the recording.
5. If the children are not capable of writing a report, they may opt for an art project, either to replace a written report or to aid them in an oral report. Art projects might include a painting, panorama, sequenced mural, model.

FIGURE 24
Reading their group's story

Once the interest groups have been formed, it is the teacher's responsibility to move freely from one group to another to see that everything is going well and to offer assistance when needed. For example, children working in an interest group may make errors in their writing. The teacher will then give skill instruction to a group that was formed because of special interest and not because of a special skill need.

Social Groups.   Social groups are formed when friends work together to accomplish a purpose. Promoting friendship is not the purpose of these groups, but working together with friends is an extra bonus.

Total-Class Group.   This story illustrates how a total-class group can work successfully. Several children in a first-grade class had been writing stories using such words as *Phoenix, telephone,* and *Philippines.* They were spelling their words phonetically using the letter *f* instead of the digraph *ph.*

One boy remarked, "Say, did you know that *ph* sounds like an *f?* I have a word that has a *ph* right in the middle of it. Several other kids in here have words that start with a *ph* and they all sound like an *f.* We all talked about it with the teacher the other day."

Special Projects.   Special-project groups are formed for the purpose of doing a "job that must be done," such as putting the art or library corner together, arranging seats for a film, straightening up the science corner, or arranging a display. In other words, there is some specific task that must be done, and working together as a group or committee is the "frosting" for the work. The amount of time a teacher spends with such a group depends on the purpose of the group. Some groups require only a moment for the teacher to tell them what task they will do. However, if skills are involved (as in writing the words on a poster), the group may need ten minutes of the teacher's undivided attention, and any interruptions will take their toll on learning.

Summary

This chapter is devoted to the word breakdown skills (usually called *word analysis*) and to grouping.

These notes summarize our thoughts on word analysis. We do not feel that a list of reading skills is necessary, even though there are some that are useful. Our objection to such lists is that they do not distinguish between skills which must be taught directly and skills which simply happen; for example, comprehension is a skill that cannot be taught, but will occur of its own accord. Furthermore, direct teaching is effective only on elements of word recognition.

Our perspective on grouping can be simply summarized. Groups are temporary; they are usually organized on a day-to-day basis, and children come and go according to their needs. Some children may be members of more than one group. The main points to remember are:

1. Groups formed on the basis of common need or interest.
2. Groups disbanded when the need or interest is satisfied.
3. Each group member should understand the purpose of the group.

5

Independent Activities

This chapter will present classroom management schemes within which teachers can work directly with one child or a small group. Teachers who use preplanned, prepared materials don't have any trouble keeping other pupils busy while they work with individuals or small groups. Our point of view is that teachers must feel comfortable with whatever operation they are carrying out, but if that operation is only a time-killing, noneducative activity, we want teachers to face that fact honestly. Workbooks by themselves don't educate; prepared material by itself doesn't educate. What does educate is the realization on the part of the pupil that a given activity will teach him something.

For example, a teacher might point out to a child on Monday that he is not making his letter *A* legibly. In a well-run, educative classroom, that pupil will respond to the suggestion, take his next free period, and *choose* to practice his letter *A*. Working problems of math, recopying writing, and finishing up the model of the space ship can be activities that children realize they can teach themselves *to* themselves.

This independence on the pupil's part is really the basis of independent activities. We asked the question then, *"What do the rest of the children do?"* Too often, the answer is, "They must be busy"—even if busy with ineffective, time-killing workbooks.

Yet the truth is that they *must* be busy. If they are not, the teacher becomes a police officer and not an instructor. This problem of indepen-

119

dent activity is perhaps the most frequent "panic" question raised by teachers about informal open-structure classrooms. Certainly those teachers who make every pupil do the same thing at the same time have no such worries. They *know* what everyone is doing! But—and what a big qualification this is—the sacrifice of child morale in learning, in schooling, in what is sensible about education is enormous. Classrooms need not be silent, nor need they be uproarious. Speech, talk, and communication are major resources which the teacher can use in many ways. Yet some teachers do panic at the thought of every child doing something different; these are the teachers we want to help in this chapter.

Planning for Independent Activities

During some part of the day, the teacher will probably want to work with individuals or even small groups. In order for a teacher to do this, she must be able to work with as little interference as possible.[1] The teacher must see to it that the other children are being occupied with some independent activities of their own choice.

In planning the independent activities for the day, it might be advisable for the teacher to choose activities based on the following criteria:

1. Will the independent activity require the child to engage in productive thinking?
2. Will the independent activity allow freedom of expression?
3. Will the independent activity use individual talents and skills?
4. Will the independent activity create new meanings out of old?
5. Will the independent activity provide practice in learning the kind of control which frees one to work productively?
6. Will the independent activity stretch the mind toward the unknown?
7. Will the independent activity result in personal satisfaction to the learner?[2]

There are, of course, tricks to every trade. The trick, or the secret, to helping a room full of children to educate themselves through self-chosen projects lies in centers of interest. Although there are all kinds of commercial centers of interest, we will deal here only with centers of interest built upon pupil choice.

---

[1] David H. Kahl and Barbara J. Gast, *Learning Centers* (Encino, California: I.C.E.D., 1974).

[2] Helen Fisher Darrow and R. Van Allen, *Independent Activities for Creative Learning* (New York: Teachers College, Columbia University, 1961), pp. 3-4.

Independent Activities Are Not "Seatwork"

Independent activities are not to be confused with "seatwork." Granted, there are classrooms in which children are working on their own while the teacher is working with a small group; this is commonly the case in classes using a basal approach where children are grouped according to reading ability. However, in such classrooms, the teacher has to do a few things in order to get the chldren working by themselves. First of all, she needs to have persuaded children to do their work quietly. Second, if there are no workbooks, instructions for the work must be written on the board in the morning before children come into the classroom. Third, different assignments must be planned for each group. (With different abilities, you have to provide work for different abilities, of course!) Fourth, children must understand what is to be accomplished during seatwork time. Fifth, each person will need materials.

In the program we believe in, the teacher's role changes from that described above. Again, it is important to remember that children don't run themselves; the teacher's presence is not to be minimized but, rather, enhanced. The teacher's job becomes one requiring much more physical, emotional, intellectual, and psychological energy. Teachers must continuously be on their toes, aware of *all* children in the classroom, and prepared to offer guidance whenever necessary. Even though this seems so much easier to describe than to inspire, once independent activities get going, a marvelously self-sufficient, self-reliant class develops. Elements of persuasion, preparation, variety of assignments, giving directions, and finding right material for children, which were necessary in ability-based groups using teacher-imposed material, are all taken care of in a self-chosen program. Teachers do not need to persuade or threaten children to finish their work quietly, nor do they need concocted jobs that stretch out classroom time.

Choice Boosts Morale

In a self-chosen program, the child has chosen the activity because it is of interest to him and, therefore, he will *want* to do it. Teachers will not have to write long and varying assignments on chalkboards, for the children feel that the classroom is theirs, and they will come knowing what work they need to do. Because the children have been working in an environment where each chooses his own word, story, and/or book, they understand individual differences. They are working in an environment where differences are accepted. If many possible classroom activities are written on the board, they are there because the children choose to do them and not because some children are less able than others to do certain activities. Teachers will not need to spend large amounts of time giving directions; directions will be indicated by the job. Each child, better than anyone else, will know what he wants to do; he will have learned to carry on.

Once a child has decided what to do, he will need to decide how to achieve his end product. The teacher can be most helpful at this point. She can make suggestions and/or talk through the project with the child. The child will have the opportunity to clear his own thinking and, at the same time, will have the teacher's guidance to expand his thinking. The teacher will not need to run around looking for the right material for the children to use; it is the job of the children to choose their own material. Arranging classrooms in interest centers will facilitate children's self-sufficiency. Once the child is clear on what he is doing and has his material, he can begin his work.

When Does It All Start?

Not surprisingly, a child can start independent activity with a key word. Children at this age level are perfectly capable of working independently; teachers forget children have been playing independently before they even start school. When they do start school, the situation requires their being watched over and directed. They come to feel dependent upon their teacher. Too often, they come to think that school is not a place to think creative thoughts but, rather, a place to sit and think only about what they have been told to think. This kind of thinking is not based on interest, hence the prime element for learning is missing.

On the other hand, children can be working independently at this age through the many activities suggested in chapter two, "Key Vocabulary." With only their one daily word, they can choose one of many activities using that word. From here, children can soon move into choosing an activity to fit a book they have read—making a mobile, illustrating certain parts, writing something.

As children have been giving their own key words and from these words writing their own stories and books, the new activity which they want to work on comes from any and all of these activities. The word *independent* implies two meanings in this program: the activity is self-chosen and is accomplished by the children themselves. Independence thus becomes one of the ultimate goals toward which the teacher guides the child. Make no mistake; teacher-made assignments are independently done, too, but the philosophies behind personalization and imposed tasks are at opposite ends of a continuum.

To choose independently requires enough teacher support for success. The child who feels insecure finds great difficulty in undertaking something on his own without knowing what is expected. The child who has been continuously harassed in school will not feel able to do something on his own unless he knows there is aid near by. On the other hand, the child who has been given choices in school work will undertake independent tasks with very little difficulty. He has been encouraged and guided in his own thinking, and can now feel confident that what he has thought of is worth doing.

Interest Centers

Sometimes the term *interest center* is confused with *learning center*. Of course, learning takes place in both. But we propose interest centers that are distinguished by *child-chosen* activities from learning centers, which are defined by *teacher-assigned* activities.

To assign "work" means that the "work" must be collected and somehow evaluated by the teacher who made the assignment. Thus, the activity is motivated by the threat of an *extrinsic* reward—a grade or a mark on whatever has been done. In addition, when teachers assign things for children to do on their own, the tendency is to provide checklists or workbook exercises on the false hope that these will teach the child some pearl of wisdom. We believe this is nonsense and offer ways to manage a classroom with centers that are intrinsically valuable and offer the children challenging and stimulating tasks. The extent that such centers hold interest is the extent to which the motivation is intrinsic. We hold intrinsic motivation of prime importance to all teaching and learning.

In an interest center success can be measured by the teacher's ability to utilize the center in linking the child and the subject. The competent teacher encourages observation, wide participation, and individuality in the use of centers. She entices students to utilize the variety of ideas found in an interest center to enrich learning by investigating those ideas in greater depth cooperatively and/or individually. The teacher asks herself, "What will this activity teach by itself that I cannot teach?"

The teacher needs to realize that every student will not be activated to learning by the same interest object; thus, she should make available abundant and varied activities. Interest centers should contain enough of the familiar so that a child will feel secure; yet, at the same time, they should offer enough of the unfamiliar to promote curiosity. Frequent changes to add new things to see and manipulate keeps interest at its peak.

These centers have been found useful because they allow children to occupy themselves with minimum of adult supervision.

1. Book Center
2. Writing Center
3. Science Center
4. Materials Center
5. Arts and Crafts Center
6. Talk Center

7. Sensory Image Center
8. Audio-Visual Center
9. Play Center
10. Dream Center
11. Activity Center

Following is a detailed presentation of what these centers might offer.

A Book Center.   First and foremost, there must be one part in the room where all library, basal, supplementary, and reference books are kept. Within this corner, there must be a great deal of reading material; an individualized reading program cannot succeed without a variety of reading matter on hand. For example:

1. Books written or typed and illustrated by children.
2. A section of factual books, which could be stocked with a set of encyclopedias, dictionaries, and science and non-fiction trade books.
3. A section of basal readers—from as many publishers and levels as possible.
4. A library section stocked with a variety of well-selected fictional storybooks that are changed frequently. (A minimum of three books for every child should be included.)
5. Children's magazines (*Child's Life, Highlights for Children, Golden Magazine*) and adult magazines (*Life, McCall's, Sports Illustrated*).
6. Local and national newspapers.

The books, magazines, and newspapers should be arranged so that the youngsters can easily find what they need. Books can be arranged either alphabetically, categorically, or in classrooms of older children, by the Dewey Decimal System.

Furniture in this center should include bookshelves, a table with chairs, a rug, throw pillows on which children can sit and read, some plants to add to the environment, and, perhaps, a card catalogue to which the children can turn when they want to look up specific books or topics. Each of these pieces of furniture might be obtained from school storage rooms, attics, or second-hand stores; looks aren't crucial—as long as a chair can hold a child or two. The presence of these kinds of furnishings adds to both the atmosphere of the reading corner and the child's attitude toward reading.[3]

A Writing Center. This center is where lovely, new, long, sharp pencils and stacks of nice, clean paper beckon those who have a good story to write or an important letter to send. Stamps, envelopes, and even a typewriter should be a part of every classroom's writing center. As many typewriters as possible should be provided for children to use in writing their own words and stories. A supply of large chart paper plus plenty of other kinds of paper should be available for the children to use. Individual 12" × 24" chalkboards made from masonite and painted with chalkboard paint provide a very real means for attracting the children's interest.

A Science Center. A number of observational tasks can be set up in this center. Children can use magnifying glasses to study turtles, snails, plants. A microscope with clear plastic holders, a small telescope, a globe, maps, star charts, potting soil, peat pots—anything children could use to study plants, animals, stars should be provided. Many supplies can be obtained at little or no cost. Children can build terrariums and aquariums, plant seeds, grow mold, keep small animals. Both teachers and children can bring in many things—seeds, insects, plants, anything that can be found in the school neighborhood or their own backyard.

A Math Center. It is in this area that children should have a place to manipulate materials, particularly those materials involved in mathematics. Cuisenaire rods, blocks, tins cans, and measuring devices of all sorts should be placed in a specific spot. Homemade mathematical devices are easy to make and inexpensive to acquire. The thrust toward inquiry and discovery in such a corner is educative in the best sense of the word.

An Arts and Crafts Center. This corner provides a place for work with paints, clay, and other wet media. Adequate wash-up facilities (a pail works fine) should be near by. It is also a place for use of colored chalk, crayons, and other dry media, along with construction paper, scissors, paste, and all other necessary implements. Many kinds of paper of different sizes, shapes, and colors may be used, and clay, crayons, and discarded materials are thus made easily accessible to children. The center could be located near a display board and shelves so that the children may display their work.

---

[3]See Chapter 6, "Children and Books," for additional discussion.

Materials that can be used in construction can also be in this corner: wood, nails, hammers, and saws are fine tools, but ground rules for safety and noise must be set up if they are included. Erector sets, Lincoln logs, and blocks can have a place in this center if the children prefer to have them here rather than in another spot in the classroom.

A Talk Center. This center provides an area where small groups of children can sit on chairs, rugs, or old pillows, and talk. Here, they can show each other the treasures they have brought from home which the class as a whole had so little time to appreciate at the beginning of the school day. This center can also be a place to which the teacher can banish two disagreeing youngsters to "talk it out." Excessively loud talking, of course, simply must be forbidden, but in an informal classroom, a place for discussion—whether with or without the teacher—can be a fine spot.

In using this corner, the teacher may find that many children need to be encouraged to take part in conversations. To remedy this situation, the teacher can encourage the children to discuss objects which she has placed in this center in a "secret sack." In other instances, the children can think of what the "secret" object might be and prepare to tell the teacher all about it at a later time.

A cassette tape recorder is a fine piece of equipment for this center. Often when children have finished their work they can go to some relatively private place with the recorder and an inexpensive cassette of short duration, and offer what ever private or public thoughts they wish.[4]

A Sensory-Image Center. In this center is placed an assortment of real objects that can be grouped easily as things to touch and feel (pieces of string, sandpaper), to smell (cologne, flowers), to hear, or to taste. The teacher labels a bag or box for each scent and has the children sort the objects and place them in the proper container.

Another exercise involves the use of home-made puzzles. Acquiring duplicates of full-page, colored pictures from magazines or extra or used reading books, the teacher or children mount one copy of each picture on heavy cardboard and cut it into large, simple pieces. The duplicate is mounted on a large envelope in which the puzzle pieces can be stored.

Objects can be placed in a cloth bag or a brightly colored sock. The children then tell what is in the bag or sock by feeling the shape of the object.

A mystery box also offers an opportunity for sensory activity. This box is constructed of cardboard boxes of various sizes and covered with con-

---

[4]Lewis Smith and Glenn Morgan, *Communications Skills through Authorship.* (Lewiston, Idaho: Lewiston Public Schools, 1973).

tact paper or paint. A hole is cut in the box large enough for a child to get his hand in so that he can try to identify the objects that he feels. The box should be placed on a table with a sign saying "Guess What Is in This Box." If the children can write, they should write their guesses or a story about what they feel. The group as a whole can listen to the stories or guesses. Objects should be changed frequently.

A textures comparison exercise can be conducted by placing materials of different textures in different boxes (sandpaper, cut-up cellophane, silk, crumpled foil, pine cone, dry leaves, feather). A sign should be placed near the boxes saying "How Does It Feel?"

To stimulate the children's sense of smell and to provide high interest and incentive, the teacher can paint containers or cover them with paper so that the children must guess the contents of each container by its odor. If a liquid is used, a piece of cotton should be inserted in the container to prevent evaporation. Here are some ideas for interesting smells: peppermint, vanilla, a bar of soap, extracts of any kind, onion, perfume, orange peels, apple slices.

An Audio-Visual Center.   In this section, a selection of tapes, records, read-along books, and filmstrips can be placed for the children to play individually or in small groups.

Such a listening post could include records, a tape player, tapes, and a tape recorder. Earphones could be included for individual listening. First-graders can learn to operate the tape recorder independently so that they can work on their spelling or oral reading. From a large reel of tape, the teacher can cut smaller sections and wind them on a small reel so that each child will have an individual tape with which to work.

An audio-visual center equipped with tapes, records, read-along books, and filmstrips provides an enriching learning experience in any room. Most first-grade children can learn to operate the machines independently so that they can use them alone or in small groups.

A Play Center.   This center is called a "Wendy House" in the British Infant Schools. A play center is almost a must so that children have a place where they are free to "play house." They can move about, use dishes, blocks, "grown-up" clothes, and indulge in many kinds of activities.

A Dream Center.   Children, particularly those in high-tension communities and large cities, appreciate a place where they can escape, yet still be protected by the knowledge that they are part of the classroom. Such a place can be a quiet spot made by using a huge packing box, like one in which a piano or an organ is shipped. In this kind of a closed-in, tiny room can be placed a rocker or a cot. The children themselves can bring objects to look at or play with while they are relaxing. Often, teachers who provide such a spot find that a sign-up sheet is needed so that children can take turns being quiet and alone.

An Activity Center. Because there are literally hundreds of activities possible in a classroom, a place is needed to store equipment and organize the directions for these activities, even if the actual activities are to be carried on in a different place. Sometimes directions are not vital in terms of intrinsic learning, but the teachers' comfort level, especially when the day is long and exhausting, is a necessary consideration. Hence, even though the following suggestions might not be relevant to the major purposes of learning, they are included for the important purpose of increasing teacher serenity. They are often a kind of make-work-drill that can be fun, time-killing, and even a kind of mildly competitive activity. Interestingly, the comfort of the teacher can stem from different sources; witness one of the project people who said, "I thought it was the children that needed the basal readers and the workbooks. But I have found out that I was the one that needed them."

So, for what they are worth, we now offer a miscellany of activities:

1. *Sorting Animal Cards.* The teacher can cut out pictures of chickens, ducks, and other animals and paste them on file cards. Then put the cards in three or more packs and let the children sort them out according to the kind of animal shown on the card.

2. *Jigsaw Puzzles.* From copies of reading books, the teacher can cut pictures of three or four-part picture stories into pieces. Then paste the pictures on file cards and shuffle them in an envelope. The child can arrange the cards on the ledge of the chalkboard or on his desk so that he can use the cards to help him to tell or write a story.

3. *Matching Pairs.* The teacher can cut out pictures that are in some way associated with one another. Then paste each picture on a sheet of paper and place the picture which is associated with it in an envelope. The children match the pictures and tell how they could be used as paired objects.

4. *Finishing a Story.* From magazines, the teacher can clip out illustrations that show children or family groups in situations in which it appears that something is about to happen. These illustrations are passed to the children who then make drawings of what they think will happen next.

5. *Matching Initial Sounds.* The teacher can locate large pictures of detailed backgrounds (kitchen, living room, family room, playground) in which there are several objects whose names begin with a particu-

FIGURE 25
Playing a word and counting game

lar sound. Circle one of the objects and let the child place markers over all of the other objects that he can find whose names begin with the same sound as the word circled.

Detailed Activities for Teachers Who Need Them

The following section contains a description of activities organized around the various centers of interest. Some readers may not need these extensive lists, which have been culled from hundreds of hours of working with teachers and which may be somewhat repetitive in nature. But be that as it may, the list is for the teacher who feels a need for concrete suggestions to help in implementing an individualized reading program.

This section is offered to help teachers see the wide variety of activities that can be incorporated into regular reading programs on either a group or an individual basis. In most cases, the activities that follow are ones that a child or a small group of children can do on an independent level while their teacher is busy with individual conferences or skill groups.

The activities have been grouped around a list of centers of interest. This list is intended to serve as a source of suggestions for things to do with *some* of the books children have read. (We do not recommend that teachers insist that children do something for each and every book they read.) Determining the actual use of these activities is left entirely with the classroom teacher. She is the only one who really knows which activities are best suited for age level of her students.

The way in which the teacher incorporates these activities can also vary. For instance, she can use this list as a personal reference. Should her students appear to be having difficulty in deciding upon something to do during reading time, she can refer to this section and make some suggestions from the list. When first implementing an individualized reading program, the teacher might want to write a few of these suggestions on the board at the start of the reading period. She can then discuss these possibilities and let the students have the option of choosing one or two of the activities. Hence, she starts students on the road to independent work. A prepared list of suggestions offers a number of ways in which these activities can be useful to the teacher. One is to prepare a mimeographed list of activities, one for each child and one to be tacked up somewhere in the classroom. In this manner, the children can refer to the list during reading time if they are wondering what to do. Another is to prepare a card file that would be categorized according to the kind of activity (i.e., all art activities in one section, all writing activities in another, etc.). In this manner, if a child feels like doing some kind of art work for a book, he merely goes to that section in the box and thumbs through until he finds an activity that appeals to him. By the same token, if a child should think of an activity that isn't in the box, he can write it up on another index card and include it in the suggested activity box. The file box then becomes a continually growing box of suggestions. Again, the manner in which the teacher chooses to use this list is left to her discretion.

Using Old Readers

Instead of throwing away old primers and readers for older children, the teacher can use them creatively by having children flip through them until they come to a picture that appeals to them. Each child then brings this picture to the teacher for a "talk out." The print is covered with a blank label. The child sits beside the teacher who has a typewriter or a black marker at hand. The dialogue should go something like this:

Teacher: What made you decide to bring this picture to talk about?

Child: Cuz I got a dog something like this here one—only my dog is black.

Teacher: What does he do?

Child: He likes to fight cats.

Teacher: What do you do about it?

Child: Nothing much, except I try to get him to quit, cuz we have a cat, and I like cats too.

Teacher: If a cat and a dog do get to fighting, who usually wins?

Child: Oh, cats do! They slap with their claws, and the dogs howl and run!

Teacher: What's your dog's name?

Child: I call him Jocko. That belongs for a monkey, but my dog is kind of a monkey anyway.

Teacher: Tell me more.

Child: Oh, he does crazy things—even tries to climb trees, only he can't.

Teacher: Well, since you have a dog that chases cats, you must be the guy on the leash in the picture—right?

Child: Yeah! I wanna be him!

Teacher: OK, now tell me just what you want to say to Jocko to make him come away from the cat.

Child: Jock, you big dum-dum, cut it out!

Teacher: That is just what we will write on this page on top of the label.

The teacher can move from here for the development of good oral reading skills of learning that "j" in Jocko is like its name and that other words start the same way—*jello, Jill,* and *Jack,* etc.[5]

Reading Center

The following activities are suggested for the child to use in the reading center:

1. Using key words.
2. Having the child say the word, trace it, write it, and spell it.
3. Making experience charts.
4. Having at his disposal many books to look at.
5. Keeping all books together—basals, texts, resource, library, and workbooks.
6. Arranging alphabet cards with holes to string them in correct order.
7. Making his own picture book and labeling the pictures in it.
8. Making a picture from a favorite story and telling about it.
9. Making dioramas about a good story.

---

[5]Courtesy of Eldon Gran, Rapid City Schools, South Dakota. The actual words on the page from the primer that the child showed the teacher were "Stop it, Gus. Stop it!" This child's language is infinitely richer.

10. Retelling a story by making pictures of it.
11. Making a cover for a book.
12. Composing a story about a picture of the student which the teacher has taken.
13. Writing a diary.
14. Writing his own books for others to read.
15. Labeling books he has read or heard by subject—animal, fairy tale, science.
16. Keeping his own dictionary.
17. Making a question sheet or card about the story he has read. This card should be clipped to the end of the story for the next reader to answer the question.

Reading and Writing Activities

Secret Orders. On a sheet of paper, the teacher writes a short order such as "Stand up and count to five." The paper is then folded and inserted into an envelope. The envelope does not necessarily need to be sealed. The teacher can either address the envelope to specific children or leave it blank. The following are suggestions for short orders:

1. Walk around the room.
2. Go to the board and write your name.
3. Stand up and jump three times.
4. Take the board eraser and give it to a boy in the class.
5. Go look out the window.
6. Sit at the teacher's desk.
7. Skip to the back of the room.
8. Hop on your right foot to the pencil sharpener.
9. Raise your right hand.
10. Stoop down.
11. Whistle a song.
12. Hum a tune.
13. Go to the cloak room and get your coat.
14. Hand a piece of chalk to some girl in the room.

All other envelopes should be placed in a box (a shoe box is good enough). While the children are sitting in their seats, the box is passed around and each child draws out an envelope. The child opens the envelope and secretly reads the order. He then refolds it and puts it back into the envelope, being sure that no one has seen the order. Some children may have difficulty in reading their order. In this case, the teacher will have to help with the words; however, another child can be used for this task if the one needing help is willing.

Now that everyone has an order and the children are ready to play, the teacher starts out by explaining that each one will be given a chance to carry out his order. Once the order is carried out, the class will try to guess what the pupil's order was. If the teacher wishes to not have the whole class participate, a group or even partners can proceed in the above fashion. Recording the guessing of the order on the chalkboard can reinforce reading and writing skills.

Writing Original Number Stories. Writing original number stories aids youngsters in learning how to solve arithmetic problems. Writing a good number story makes the following demands upon its author:

1. Understanding of the meaning of the problem.
2. Choosing data pertinent to the problem.
3. Discriminating between a sensible number story and one that isn't.
4. Knowing the methods to be used in solving a problem.
5. Having the skills needed to make the correct computations.

At what age can children be expected to create their own number stories? Making up original problems is often one phase of the arithmetic study for children as early as first grade. At first, the children should be provided with counters (bottle caps, styrofoam "peanuts," crayon stubs) for solving problems which the teacher gives. Later, they may be asked to make up problems similar to the ones given. Children's problems are usually taken from their own experiences. For example, the child might say:

Three boys are absent today.
Four girls are absent, too.
How many children are absent?

I had six sticks of gum.
I gave two to George.
How many do I have left?

Often, a child solves the problem with his counters as he states it.

The authors have seen problems solved through the use of pictures. The children line (first graders usually fold) their papers once vertically and three or four times horizontally. This acquisition of a large space for each story precludes crowding. Often, the teacher draws a similar "paper" on the chalkboard or a large piece of newsprint. Then she may say, "In the top row in the left box (space, block, etc.) write your name."

Sue A.	

Then, she may continue, "Listen to the story:

Marie has two pieces of candy.
Peter has three pieces of candy.
How many pieces do both children have?"

The teacher may then ask, "Who would like to make a picture for this story in this box?" (She points to the space at the right in the top row of drawing on the blackboard.) "I'll say the problem again and you show it by drawing pictures on your papers. How many candies did you draw? Is five the answer to the problem? Write the answer in the same box."

Sue A.	

The lesson may continue with similar problems.
Later, when youngsters are able to work with numbers, they may write the algorithm as well as draw the pictures for each story.

Sue A.	● ● ● 3 ● ● +2 5

When the children no longer need the help of semiconcrete representations, they may write only the algorithm in each space as the teacher gives the problem.

Sue A.	$\begin{array}{r} 3 \\ +\,2 \\ \hline 5 \end{array}$

After several such lessons, the children should be ready to write original problems. The project may be introduced by the teacher's saying, "Today we are going to write and illustrate our own number stories." To help the children start on their stories, the teacher may add, "You may use your paper for the story. I will give you a paper (perhaps 2″ × 4″) for each illustration and a paper clip so you can clip the picture to your problem. (Having separate papers for the illustrations helps children to arrange pictures and problems without crowding.) I'll write on the board some words you may need help with. If you do not know how to write a word that you want to use and do not see it on the board, raise your hand and I'll come to you." (The children may also have access to their own word list or box.) The teacher writes the more frequently used words (bought, spent, gave, more, how much, cents) on the board.

Children should be encouraged to write algorithms for their problems. Later, when they show that they understand the abstract representation of the problem and no longer need drawings to help them, the drawings may be dispensed with and the algorithms used alone.

The following are original problems written, illustrated, and colored with crayons by second-grade children.

I had seven cents.
I found five cents.
How much do I have now?

Chris

Chris	7 + 5 ――― 12

In the following problem, the child showed the algorithm only.

I had four cookies.
I gave two cookies to Laura.
How many do I have left?

That problem-writing can be fun is evident in the following problems from the interesting situations described, the sense of humor revealed, and the attempt to make them difficult for other children to solve.

I was writing to my father.
I wrote first Dear Daddy.
How many letters are in Daddy?

Cheryl
Age 5

I looked into a herd of horses.
I counted twenty legs.
Two horses walked away and
Eight legs went with them.
How many legs were left?

Dana
Age 12

Making up a story about spending their allowances, adding to savings, or planning for a class trip or project is always interesting to children. When writing number stories or original problems, enough time should be given for the children to share their original problems with the class. These original problems can be collected and put in a class scrapbook, or each child may make an individual scrapbook to take home.

Building a Word List with Same Initial Sounds

The teacher will often discover that several children need help on the same skill in word analysis. Word lists can be constructed for these children that will help develop awareness of the needed sound. The word lists, however, should be an outgrowth of the children's own work. The teacher should select a word that has been used in an experience story that day, write the word on the board, and then say it. She would then ask the children to look through the story to see if they can find any other words that begin with the same sound as the one written on the board. She should be sure to check through the story first to make sure there are other words with the same initial sound.

Once similar words have been found in the story, the children should be encouraged to think of other words on their own. Every word should be written on the board. Teacher and class continue in this manner until the children are unable to think of any other words. Then, the list of words is read to the class in the order written. Each child should be allowed to read back the words individually. He may read the entire list of words or just a portion; the decision of how much to read should be based on his wishes. Finally, the teacher should make a permanent copy of all the words mentioned during this activity.

Building a List of Words Which Have the Same Endings

The same techniques as were used for beginning sounds can be used for building a list of ending sounds. After the lists have been completed, the children should be allowed to add endings to the other words in order to see how the endings affect the structure of different words. These are examples of rules which the children themselves have come up with:

1. Words ending with an *e* must have the final *e* dropped before adding an ending.
2. Words that have short vowel sounds before the last consonant will need to have the last consonant doubled before adding an ending.

The words falling into these patterns could be categorized under a pattern heading such as "Dropping the *e* Words" and "Doubling the Last Consonant Words." The children may wish to make their own copy of these words to be either filed in a word box or taken home to show their parents. The teacher should make a permanent copy of these words to be placed in the room for future reference.

Building Related Word Lists

In this exercise, the teacher writes a word on the board that relates to the present conversation or is taken from an experience story of the day. She should try to select a word that is known by all children, and then ask the children to say the words that come to mind when they think of the word on the board. For example, if the lead word is "strong," children may think of such words as "Superman," "mighty," "healthy," "powerful," "muscles."

The purpose of the activity is to find as many words as possible that are related in some way. In other words, a list of synonyms is built with the class without a definition for "synonym" actually being given.

Word and Book Activities

1. *Finding words* that have the same initial sound.
2. *Finding words* that have the same ending.
3. *Putting words* from the experience story in alphabetical order.
4. *Finding the syllables* in words from a story book, day's experience story, or the chalkboard.
5. *Making an alphabet booklet* using pictures from a magazine.
6. *Making a booklet of drawings.*
7. *Making a booklet* using magazine pictures relating to one topic. For example, a child might want to cut out pictures about different cars, paste each picture on a sheet of drawing paper and write a short sentence about the picture.
8. *Making a booklet* about one's self, showing the different activities during a day, week, year. These booklets might be about:
   a. a child's family.
   b. incidents that occurred on the way to school.
   c. incidents that occurred in school.
   d. playing with friends.
   e. going shopping.
9. *Writing a letter* to a friend (with the understanding that the letter will be mailed).
10 *Drawing a picture* about something one has seen and writing a sentence or two explaining the drawing.
11. *Making animals or people out of clay,* then using the figures to tell a story. (The manipulation of figures helps children verbalize.)
12. *Making an animal* of one's own choice with play-dough.

13. *Making an item* of interest using either clay or play-dough. Again, these items should be used as helps in telling or writing a story.
14. *Covering coffee cans* with contact paper. The end product can serve as a storage container for the pencils, scissors, crayons.
15. *Labeling* the coffee cans.
16. *Cutting out* the cutouts found in a book.
17. *Making a diorama* of the cutouts.
18. *Putting a puzzle together* by yourself.
19. *Putting a puzzle together* with a friend.
20. *Playing a game* with friends.
21. *Making a diorama* using drawing paper, magazines, newspaper, cardboard.
22. *Cutting out large letters,* such as those found in newspaper headlines, and pasting them on stiff paper or cardboard. The letters can also be used to make an alphabet book, a book of similar words, a dictionary of the child's own words.
23. *Finding words* from an experience story in a trade book and doing something else with the words, such as writing a different sentence or story about them.
24. *Making holiday decorations* for the classroom using "found" materials, such as foil, pretty weed shapes dipped in paint, egg cartons.
25. *Writing a note* to someone at home or in class.
26. *Making something* with drawing paper.
27. *Reading a book* with a friend.
28. *Arranging the books* in the library according to the alphabetical order of the author's names.
29. *Arranging the books* in the library according to their topics, such as *Poetry, Space, Cowboys.*
30. *Selecting some words for a race* among the class or a few friends to see who can find them fastest in the dictionary.
31. *Taking turns* with friends being a writer and an artist. The children should ask the teacher if the class all can do this together some time.
32. *Holding a word exchange.* An exchange for discarded words works wonders. If a child does not know his word, the teacher replies, "That doesn't make any difference. Just put it in the exchange box." Children may go through the exchange box any time and, if they find words they want and know, they may add that word to their stockpile. If they "lost" a word and cannot find one to replace it, they may get another one from the teacher.
33. *Decorating two large coffee cans* and labeling one "Things I Like" and the other "Things I Don't Like." The children can write stories

about the things they like or don't like and place them in the appropriate can for others to read. They do not have to sign them.

Book Covers

After the children have read more than one book either outside of class or during an individual reading time in class, a discussion can be held about each child's favorite book. Book covers can be utilized for these classroom discussions. The class can examine some of the covers together, noting the things usually found on a book cover (title, picture, summary of the story, author). As an outgrowth of this discussion, the teacher could suggest making book covers for favorite books.

The child can now write a summary of his favorite story, telling enough of the story to interest others in reading it. These summaries should be checked over together before rewriting them on the covers themselves.

For the actual cover, manila, construction, or similar paper may be used. With a paper cutter, the teacher can cut the paper to fit the book, leaving enough paper on either side to tuck in as the flap. The summary can be written either on the back of the cover or on the flap. (The back provides more room.) With crayons, the title and a picture can then be drawn on the front. The finished book covers can be used on a bulletin board to stimulate further reading and/or shown individually to the class.

Additional Activities

1. *Making pictures and posters* with crayons, chalk, paint, paper, cloth.
2. *Experimenting with color* using all of the above materials and more.
3. *Arranging displays,* exhibits, bulletin boards.
4. *Decorating the room* with friezes, panels, curtains, beauty corners.
5. *Constructing maps,* dioramas, table scenes, buildings, means of transportation.
6. *Making folders,* booklets, logs, slides for record keeping.
7. *Designing* and making simple costumes and props for plays.
8. *Making dolls,* puppets, movie machines, shadow plays for performances.
9. *Making gifts* for family, friends, school bazaars, social service agencies.
10. *Spinning,* carding, weaving, and enriching textiles.
11. *Printing programs,* invitations, table decorations for festivities.

12. *Constructing equipment* for elementary science and music.
13. *Modeling figures,* animals, containers with clay and *papier-mâché.*
14. *Using wood* to make houses and small items of furniture.
15. *Utilizing discarded materials* in all kinds of experimenting.
16. *Talking about* famous paintings and sculpture.
17. *Making posters* illustrating parts of books that will interest others.
18. *Making dioramas* showing interesting scenes from books.
19. *Making comic strips* illustrating the sequence of events in a story.
20. *Retelling a story* in sequence by making pictures of it.
21. *Making clay,* soap, wood, or plaster models to illustrate characters or an event in a book.
22. *Preparing cutouts* of favorite characters to mount on bulletin board called "Friends from Books."
23. *Constructing mobiles* of favorite characters from books.
24. *Preparing movie or television shows* by drawing and pasting together scenes from books. Rolled on a broom handle, such a series of scenes can be passed through a frame cut from a packing carton.
25. *Preparing bookmarks* illustrated with a favorite part or character from a book and handing these bookmarks out to members of the class.
26. *Preparing a time line* illustrating and describing the historical sequence of events in a favorite historical novel or a biography.
27. *Preparing feltboard characters* and using a story-telling approach to present a book to the class.
28. *Preparing a bulletin board mural* with several other people who have read the same book or who have read similar kinds of books.
29. *Illustrating a certain part of a book*—the favorite, happiest, saddest.
30. *Making paper bag masks.* Each child fits a large paper bag over his partner's head, marks with a crayon the places for eyes, nose, and mouth, removes the bag, and cuts out the places marked. Any kind of design (wiggly ears, cotton eyebrows) can be put on the mask.
31. *Tearing simple shapes,* such as balls, trees, or houses, from newspapers. Drawing large pictures on the chalkboard and making border designs (repeated designs) on large sheets of paper.
32. *Making mobiles* by designing and cutting out characters and objects from a favorite story or book. These designs are attached to threads and suspended from a light fixture. This suspension causes the mobile to flutter in the air and make moving shadows against the wall.
33. *Making puppets* of story characters. The children proceed as they would in dramatizing a story. Stick puppets are easiest for little

children to make; a crayoned cardboard cutout makes a perfectly satisfactory stick puppet. They can be made by taping on a stiff cardboard strip for handling and drawing a character's face on one side of a paper bag. The top of the head should be at the closed end of the bag while both sides of the bag below the head should be slit and stuffed loosely with crumpled paper. A string tied around the bag below the head makes the puppet complete, unless yarn or string is added for the hair.

34. *Drawing or making clothes for cutouts.* Buttons, ribbons, yarn, and cotton in the crafts center boxes will give a good choice of trimmings.

35. *Modeling with clay* can teach the children how to make models that will stand up. After the models have been made, they can be painted *provided they have dried overnight.* On the third day they can be given a coat of shellac.

36. *Making bulletin board displays* by stretching lengths of bright yarn around pins and sticking them into corkboard, thus outlining a house or street. The children can then arrange rooms of cutout paper furniture or make houses on the streets.

37. *Making self-portraits* on 9" × 12" sheets of paper and pasting all pictures on large pieces of tagboard. Names may then be added to the chart by the teacher, thereby enabling children to recognize each other's names. Life-size portraits can be made by working in pairs and drawing each other's outline on large sheets of paper. Each child can finish the portrait by dressing the outline in a favorite outfit.

38. *Using left-over odds and ends*—bits of felt, paste, newsprint, wallpaper books—for arts and crafts. The children can make interesting designs or pictures to feel.

Oral Reading

Group Reading. For this activity, the class is divided into three or four groups, and each group selects a chairperson and then chooses a story from one of the books available in the library corner. After choosing, the chairperson calls on individuals to read aloud to the group. As they read, they may stop to discuss the story if someone in the group does not understand a point. Those chldren who are unable to read the story can listen and contribute to the discussion.

After completing the story, the children can report the story to the teacher in a sequential fashion, with each child telling a portion of the

FIGURE 26
Active listening

story. Or the children can describe the story on a mural. On pieces of paper eight to ten feet long, the children can paint a character and show several different situations this character was in during the story; or they can also paint the story in sequence, showing different important scenes as they were described. After the pictures are complete, they can be displayed in the classroom. One note of caution is in order: the children should not make more than three or four pictures on any one mural because it will become congested and difficult to understand.

In another activity, each child selects a part of his book to read to the class. Then the class can discuss the story and try to guess the ending before it is actually read.

Each child can read a library book that a younger child might enjoy, practice reading it well, and then arrange a time to read it to a class of younger children during their story time.

Finally, the children can make tape recordings of their stories. A group of four to six pupils can each read the part of one character. Practice reading and the actual recording can be done in the rear of the classroom or in any available space in the building.

Writing Activities to Use for Children's Books

I. Synopsis of a Story.[6]

A. What is it?

A brief account of what the reading material was about.

Example: Marshmallow

> This book tells of the friendship between a rabbit and a cat and how they got along. The book has two poems that tell of the "cons" of having a rabbit and of the "pros" of having a rabbit. Marshmallow is a little rabbit who lives in a house with a cat. At first, he lived on the opposite side of the door to the kitchen where the cat is. One day, they meet and the cat takes Marshmallow to heart like a kitten. They become very good friends and the pictures show Marshmallow getting into different things with the cat, from playing to sleeping together.

B. How might it be used?

1. To describe the whole story.
2. To describe certain chapters.
   a. best-liked
   b. least-liked
3. To describe certain characters.
   a. best-liked
   b. least-liked
   c. main character
   d. minor character
4. To give illustrations.
5. To present a point and report findings.
6. To state the theme.

---

[6]Take care that this activity is not used for book reports. Too often these serve to punish children for finishing a book.

II. Book Review

   A. What is it?

   A critical discussion of a book.

   Example: Angelo Goes to Switzerland

   The book was good because the professor made
   the story both sad and funny. Even happiness was
   added by Marie Louise and her music-making
   cows.

   B. How might it be used?

   1. To describe the whole book.
   2. To describe certain chapters.
      a. best-liked
      b. least-liked
   3. To describe certain characters.
      a. best-liked
      b. least-liked
      c. main character(s)
      d. minor character(s)
   4. To give illustrations.
   5. To state the theme.
   6. To discuss the style of the book.

III. Opinions

   A. What is it?

   What you think about the book? What is your personal evaluation?

   Example: The Lion and the Mouse

   A moral lesson is one thing that is always helpful
   to everyone at every age. *The Lion and the Mouse*
   is one of Aesop's famous fables that teaches us a
   lesson that we can use in everyday life. It shows us
   the lion, who saves a mouse's life, and the mouse,
   who in return promises that if the lion ever needs
   help, the mouse will always be available. The
   mouse finally comes to the aid of the lion and
   saves his life. The moral lesson learned is "No
   matter how small an act of kindness is, it is never
   wasted." This is a very good moral especially for

younger children. The story form and characters make it interesting for the children and a lesson is learned in return.

B. How might it be used?

   1. To evaluate the whole book.
   2. To evaluate certain chapters.
     a. best-liked
     b. least-liked
   3. To evaluate certain characters.
     a. best-liked
     b. least-liked
     c. main character(s)
     d. minor character(s)
   4. To evaluate illustrations.
   5. To evaluate the theme.
   6. To evaluate the style of the book.

IV. Booklets

A. What is it?

A book made by the child himself by putting paper together by stapling, pasting, clipping, etc.

Example:

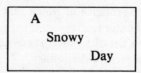

A
Snowy
Day

B. How might it be used?

   1. To rewrite the story and include pictures.
   2. To draw pictures of how characters are seen.
   3. To rewrite the story and make improvements where needed.
   4. To do a booklet on a related title.
   5. To depict certain scenes and illustrate theme.

V. Reference Book

A. What is it?

A collection of materials related to one topic.

Example:

| Cars | Engines | Chrome |

B. How might it be used?

1. If a child is interested in a particular topic (such as cars), he can read material on topic, summarize it, and put this information into a booklet form.

VI. Dictionary

A. What is it?

A book containing words placed in alphabetical order with their meanings.

Example: The Man Who Didn't Wash His Dishes

Dishes—things we use to put food on.
Hungry—wanting to eat food.
Sink—an appliance used to wash dishes or clothes.

B. How might it be used?

1. To take out difficult words and record meanings from readings.
2. To write words, their meanings, and to use words in a sentence. The sentence in which that word was found could be used in a story.
3. To make a list of science words and their meanings.
4. To start a picture-dictionary.

VII. List of Words

A. What is it?

A collection of words that are related in some way.

Example: Little Pig's Picnic

nouns	*pronouns*	*verbs*
a. pig	a. it	a. went
b. barnyard	b. she	b. find
c. supper	c. they	c. jump

B. How might it be used?

1. To write action words the children find in a book.
2. To write descriptive words they find in a book.
3. To write antonyms, homonyms, rhyming words, and synonyms found in a book.
4. To write picture words found in book.

VIII. *Character Sketch*

A. What is it?

An outline made on a character.

Example: Make Way for Ducklings
   Mike (the police officer)
   a. big   c. kind
   b. fat   d. friendly

B. How might it be used?

1. To describe certain characters.
2. To describe a best-liked character.
3. To describe a least-liked character.
4. To describe the hero.

IX. *Comments on the Illustrations*

A . What is it?

The child writes what he thinks of the pictures found in the
story.

Example: Andy and the Lion
   The illustrations in this book were beautifully displayed. The illustrations portrayed the action as it
   was taking place on each page.

B. How might it be used?

1. To prepare illustrations to story.
2. To comment on colors of illustrations.
3. To comment on lack of colors.
4. To ask if the illustrations added to the story and if so,
   how?

X. Bibliography

A. What is it?

A list of books that includes title and author.

Example: Homer Price by Robert McCloskey
Centerburg Tales by Robert McCloskey
Games of Many Nations by E.O. Harbin

B. How might it be used?

1. To list names and authors of books that the child has read.
2. To list books and then duplicate the list and distribute it to the class.
3. To list books on a certain topic.

XI. List of Ideas

A. What is it?

A thought found in the reading selection.

Example: The Fuzzy Duckling
1. Family life
   a. need for family cooperation in working together
   b. ideas of reproduction
2. Farm life
   a. different animals which are needed on a farm

B. How might it be used?

1. To make a list of ideas found in book.
2. To list ideas that are new to the child.

XII. Written Biography

A. What is it?

An account of the author's life history.

Example: Robert McClosky was born in the New England States. Both his stories and illustrations are completed with care and excellence.

B. How might you use it?

1. To write a biography on one author.
2. To make a collection of biographies.
3. To compare biography of one author with that of another.

XIII. Written Directions

A. What are they?

Instructions telling how to do something.

Example: Arts and Crafts Book

Making a Paper Bag Mask
1. Get a large paper bag.
2. Cut holes for the eyes.
3. Color on cheeks, ears, eyebrows, lips.

B. How might they be used?

1. To write directions for an experiment to show class.
2. To write directions for an experiment for the class to do.
3. To write out directions for making cake in a cookbook.

XIV. A Booklist

A. What is it?

A list of the names of books.

Example: Hercules the Gentle Giant
Hi Tom
Bozo and All the Children
Story of Alaska
Lion and the Mouse

B. How might it be used?

1. To list books according to topics.
2. To list books that were read.
3. To list books that the child wants to read.

XV. Writing a Script for TV or Radio

A. What is it?

Writing out what might be an announcement for TV or radio.

Example: Just received word that the library has received some new books. Some of the new titles are *One Morning in Maine, Old Charlie, Mike Mulligan's Steam Shovel.* If I were you, I would get to the library before these new books have all been taken out.

B. How might it be used?

1. To make an announcement of new books in the class or library.
2. To make an announcement of newly published books.
3. To write out an announcement for a book.

XVI. *Writing A Play*

A. What is it?

Story that will be told through the characters. Dialogue is written out for each character.

Example: Franklin and the King

Characters: King George III
Queen Mother
Sir Tobiase
Lord North

Scene: London, in 1774, in the king's palace.

Directions: King is pallid, nervous, and has definite qualities of indecisiveness. The Queen is stern, stately, and authoritative.

King: But, Mother, Franklin is my friend.
Mother: Franklin is your enemy. You must act now. The people are counting on you.
King: But . . . Oh, I wish . . .
Mother: No wishes. Command, George. Be a king.

B. How might it be used?

1. To put a story the children have read into play form, which could be put on for the whole class.
2. To speak the dialogue of a play into a tape recorder.

XVII. Comparison of a book to a movie

    A. What is it?

    The book is read and the movie seen. A comparison of the two is made.

    Example: 20,000 Leagues Under the Sea

        The motion picture followed the book pretty closely since the description of the book fight scenes between the giant sea squid and the corresponding fight in the movie are markedly alike.

    B. How might it be used?

      1. To tell what contribution the book makes that the movie doesn't make.
      2. To tell what contributed more, the book or movie.
      3. To compare certain scenes from book to the movie.
      4. To determine whether there was any difference in the movie from the book.
      5. To decide which the child liked better—the movie or the book.

XVIII. Making a Book Jacket

    A. What is it?

    Something catchy written on the inside of the jacket or on the back in order to attract someone's attention.

    Example: About Magnets

        1. How the different poles of the magnet attract or repel.
        2. Difference between electromagnets and regular magnets.
        3. Different shapes of magnets

    B. How might it be used?

      1. To write title and author on front (illustrator might also be included).
      2. To write on the back or inside:
        a. a review of book
        b. an advertisement

c. a teaser

d. some leading questions

XIX. Publisher's Blurb

A. What is it?

An advertisement for a book.

Example: "Let Your Fingers Do the Walking
through the Iliad"

"Fly the Friendly Sky of Whirlybird"

"Thomas Promised Pun Fun"

"Tell Harry the Dirty Dog About Dial"

B. How might it be used?

1. To advertise a book that the children have read. Advertisement can be written on a piece of paper and attached to the book.

XX. Telegram Writing

A. What is it?

A short brief statement about a book.

Example: Six Silly Fishermen

Story about six brothers who go fishing STOP
One fish gets lost STOP They forgot to count him
STOP Little boy comes along STOP He finds the
lost fish STOP

B. How might it be used?

1. In place of a summary, synopsis, review.
2. To report on a book in a brief way.
3. To send telegrams to each other about books they read.

XXI. Letter Writing

A. What is it?

A friendly letter written to someone.

Example: Dear Miss Asmer (school nurse),

> I have just finished reading a wonderful book about space. I am writing this letter to inform you that I recommend the book to you. Take the time to read *The Stars: Steppingstones into Space* by Irving Adler, and please write back to me telling me how you enjoyed the book.
>
> Thank you

B. How might it be used?

1. To write to the author of the book. Letter could be:
   a. in appreciation for book
   b. criticism of book
   c. how child felt about book
   d. what the book told child
2. To write to the teacher. Pupil pretends he is a minor character giving a first person account of main character actions in the story.
3. To write to the librarian.
4. To write to the superintendent.
5. To write to the principal.
6. To write to other teachers in the building.
7. To write to other pupils in the classroom or building.
8. To write to one of the characters.
9. To have a character in the book write to any other character from another book.

XXII. Writing Original Stories

A. What is it?

An original story rewritten from the story.

Example: Sleeping Beauty changes to *Sleeping Princess*

> Sleeping Princess was a pretty woman. She had long black hair and wore beautiful silk kimonos. She had beautiful dark skin with almond-shaped eyes. She drank a magic potion and fell asleep for a hundred days.

B. How might it be used?

1. To rewrite the story adding the children's own ideas.
2. To rewrite the story to make it say what the children would want it to say.
3. To rewrite the story to give it an entirely different twist.

XXIII. Writing Book Reports without Endings

A. What is it?

A report on a story that was read that does not include the ending.

Example: The Three Little Pigs

Once upon a time there were three little pigs who were always running away from the wolf. One day the wolf trapped all three pigs in one house. He knocked on the door and said, "_____."

B. How might it be used?

1. To swap reports and have friends add their own endings.
2. To place unfinished reports on library shelf for other people to read and try to guess what happens. If they become interested, they might want to read the book.

XXIV. Making Crossword Puzzles

A. What is it?

A puzzle that can be completed only with a knowledge of the book.

Example: Make Way for Ducklings

Down	Across
1. Mother mallard	2. Father mallard
3. One baby duckling	4. One of the baby ducks

_____
_____
_____
_____
_____

B. How might it be used?

1. To make puzzles based on characters which can be traded with friends.

    2. To make puzzles based on chapters which can be traded with friends.

    3. To make puzzles based on places named in the book that can be traded with friends.

  XXV. *One or More Paragraphs Describing any of these Parts of the Book:*

    A. The part the child liked best.

    B. The ending scene.

    C. Something that has happened to the child similar to a happening in the book.

    D. Something the child likes to do that is similar to that done in the book.

    E. The funniest part of the book.

    F. The most exciting part of the book.

    G. The setting of the book (where the story took place; the child might prepare map).

  XXVI. *Writing a New Ending to the Book*

  XXVII. *Writing a Make-believe Newspaper Article Using Information from the Book*

XXVIII. *Making a Scrapbook or a Collection of Things about the Subject of the Book; Labeling All Items and Writing a Short Descriptive Paragraph of the Most Interesting Ones*

  XXIX. *Finding Out about a Favorite Author and Writing a Brief Biography*

  XXX. *Comparing the Book with a Similar One the Child Has Read*

  XXXI. *Preparing a Diary of the Experiences of the Main Character*

  XXXII. *Setting up a Post Office in One Corner of the Room Where Children Can "Mail" Letters to Other Classmates or the Teacher*

Science Center

The following materials should be available in the Science Center:

1. magnifying glass
2. magnets
3. terrarium
4. microscope
5. aquarium

Activities for children to use in the science center include:

1. *Examining a variety of objects* (leaves, cloth, sand, wood grains) with the magnifying glass and, if possible, with a microscope.
2. *Keeping track of the weather* by keeping a class "weather calendar." Children can take turns being "weathercasters." Picture symbols can be used to record weather.
3. *Making a "seasons" book,* chart, or bulletin board display. Listing and/or illustrating weather typical for each season and naming appropriate clothing changes.
4. *Observing animal life* in a class aquarium or plant life in a class terrarium.
5. *Experimenting with magnets.* Seeing what objects magnets attract.
6. *Planting seeds* and observing growth. Measuring growth. Example: Planting beans in jar. Observing growth of roots and shoots.
7. *Studying animals*—pets, mammals, toads. Identifying characteristics, habits, food. Charting these. Making displays of information learned about the animals.
8. *Collecting objects* (seeds, shells, rocks, leaves, insects) and labeling them. Mounting them for display.
9. *Making dictionaries* of space terms with illustrations.
10. *Comparing weights* and sizes of different objects found in the classroom.
11. *Experimenting with inclined planes.*
12. *Going for a walk* around the school. Observing animals, trees, and flowers. When they have returned to the classroom, children can draw and label pictures of what they have seen. Making a booklet of these.

Materials Center

These are among the things that should be available for children to use:
1. cuisenaire rods
2. weights to balance

3. bingo
4. money games:
    a. for buying and selling things they want
    b. to play grocery store
    c. to play toy store
5. counting charts by ones, twos, fives, and tens
6. number sets for bulletin board display

   Example: 3   3 = 0   1 = 2   2 = 1   0 = 3

7. counting sticks
8. counting beads
9. abacus
10. mathematics problems made by the children for the other children
    to solve
11. tinkertoys
    1. to make line segments and add the segments
    2. to make angles and shapes

The items listed below should be available in an area where the children
can experiment with them.

1. yardstick
2. rulers
3. tape measure
4. baby bottle with ounces shown
5. thermometer
6. kitchen or baby scales
7. teaspoon
8. tablespoon
9. funnel
10. one-cup measuring cup
11. one-half cup measuring cup
12. one-fourth cup measuring cup
13. cubic-inch blocks
14. cubic-foot blocks
15. number lines

The children might try the following activities:

1. Place question cards in a box. The child draws one card and answers
   the question shown on the card.

Example: Put cold water in a glass. Use the thermometer to find the temperature. Now put hot water in a glass. What is the difference?

Other questions that might be asked include:
How long is your foot?
How long is your desk?
How many teaspoons are in a tablespoon?

2. Old milk containers can be made available for the children to use. Then the following questions can be asked:
How many pints are in a quart?
How many quarts are in a half-gallon?
How many ounces are in a pint?

The following containers must be available for this exercise:
one-half pint container
quart container
pint container
one-half gallon container
gallon container

3. Children can make calendars and find special days.

Arts and Crafts Center

The following types of equipment should be available:

1. colored chalk
2. crayons
3. finger paints
4. clay
5. sticks, wood, cardboard
6. *papier-mâché*
7. newspaper
8. magazines
9. paper bags
10. tempera paint
11. construction paper in whole pieces and scraps
12. wood
13. buttons, string, etc.
14. felt tip markers
15. white newsprint—all sizes
16. paste

The following activities are suggested for the Arts and Crafts Center:

1. *Making pictures and posters* with crayon, chalk, paint, cutout paper, cloth.
2. *Experimenting with color* utilizing all of the above materials.
3. *Arranging displays,* exhibits, bulletin boards.
4. *Decorating the room* with friezes, panels, curtains, beauty corners.
5. *Constructing maps,* dioramas, table scenes, buildings, illustrations of transportation.
6. *Making folders,* booklets, logs, slides for record keeping.
7. *Designing and making simple costumes* and props for plays.
8. *Making dolls,* puppets, movie machines, shadow plays for performances.
9. *Making gifts* for family, friends, school bazaars, social service agencies.
10. *Spinning,* carding, weaving, and enriching textiles.
11. *Printing programs,* invitations, table decorations for festivities.
12. *Constructing equipment* for elementary science and music centers.
13. *Modeling with clay* and *papier-mâché* figures, animals, containers.
14. *Using wood* to make small items of furniture and houses.
15. *Utilizing discarded materials* in all kinds of experimenting.
16. *Talking about famous paintings* and sculpture.

Talk Center

The following dramatizing activities are appropriate for the Talk Center:

1. *Preparing an illustration* and telling the story of the book to a class of younger children.
2. *Doing a pantomine* about some part of the book, with the audience trying to guess what is being portrayed.
3. *Preparing a puppet show* of a scene from the book.
4. *Dramatizing one or more scenes* from a book that a few class members have read.
5. *Writing a play* based on the book and performing it on a radio show using appropriate sound effects and props.

The following ideas for panel discussions are suggested as whole-class activities:

1. *Bringing in articles* from magazines and newspapers about authors or books the children have read.

2. *Discussing* what reading books has meant to each child, using the book he has read most recently as an example.
3. *Holding a panel discussion* on the problems faced by the main character in the book the child has just read and discussing how the character reacted to his problem.

Audio-Visual Center

The materials listed below are needed in such a center:

1. bells
2. music paper
3. piano
4. plain paper
5. radio
6. record player with earphones
7. records—all types
8. storybook-record sets
9. tape recorder with blank and prerecorded tapes

The following activities are suggested for the audio-visual center:

1. *Listening to records* of all types—popular, country-western, classical, story records, children's songs. Trying to identify what kind of music is being played or what kind of music is a child's favorite.
2. *Bringing the children's own records* from home into the classroom to use.
3. *Recording and listening to stories.* Prerecorded cassettes, either commercial or teacher-made, may be used.
4. *Playing a song* on the piano by number or letter. (Piano keys can be numbered or lettered by note.)
5. *Writing the child's own song* or melody on music paper provided.
6. *Setting a poem to music.*
7. *Playing "Name That Tune"* with a tune written down by the teacher.
8. *Trying to fill in the melody* of a song that has only the lyrics present.
9. *Using art paper and crayons* to draw designs suggested by the music on a record.
10. *Organizing a band* and performing for the class (using drums, bells, piano, triangles).
11. *Recording a song* to play for the class alone or with a friend.

12. *Presenting a medley* of songs with accompaniment.
13. *Taping various sounds* (city, animal, household sounds) and seeing if anyone can name them.
14. *Going for a walk* and writing down all of the sounds that are heard. This activity should be done at different times of the day and year.
15. *Having a friend listen* to the child's voice.

A Camera as an Assistant Teacher

Having your picture taken and even taking your own picture serves as a motivating factor for talking and writing. With such photos children can create books for themselves and others to read. These, like other original books, can become part of the library supply within the classroom.

Added to this activity is the project of developing one's own film with a homemade developing kit. The following section describes how one might go about creating such apparatus.

Obtaining and Creating the Equipment.   Cameras can be purchased at prices as low as $2.50. The less expensive brands are: Panax, Rover, Arrow, Diana, and Valiant. The usual film for these is 620 black and white. Camera stores often offer unknown brands or outdated film at considerable discounts—don't hesitate to try it.

"Black changing bags"—or "hand darkrooms" as children have called them—are sewn from forty-four inch widths of black cotton or rayon taffeta, used double thick. In use, the bags are tied lightly about the elbows with twine. Each bag requires a two-yard length which when doubled, redoubled, and stitched, makes an open-ended tube that is approximately 42 inches long by 18 inches wide.

These bags are not available in stores, but they can be made easily. Any close-woven, lightweight fabric is suitable if two thicknesses of it completely hide the light from a bare 100 watt bulb.

Some teachers have found that a box or frame-like structure inserted into the bag makes it easier for children to handle the film. Other teachers have found a frame unnecessary. A simple, cheap frame can be made of folding a 10 × 32 inch piece of corrugated cardboard into a square-shaped tube and inserting it into the bag. A piece of tape will keep the ends of the cardboard joined.

The developer described in our book is Dektol, manufactured by Eastman Kodak and widely available in camera stores. Several other manufacturers have similar universal developers in their catalogues; for instance—General Aniline Film's Vividol, Agfa's Neutol.

The chemical fixer (widely known by photographers as *hypo*) is also available from camera stores and suppliers. The least expensive kind, and the one described in *It's So Simple* . . . is sodium thiosulfate in crystal form. Most manufacturers have some form of this fixer in their catalogues.

The developing tank used by the authors of *It's So Simple* . . . is the Kodacraft Roll Film Tank, manufactured by Eastman Kodak and available wherever their products are sold. Several other developing tanks are available and would, in many cases, make good substitutes for the Kodak tank. They won't, however, work on the Lasagne principle, and they may be difficult for younger children to load. A test to determine that your students can easily load film into the particular tank is advisable.

The printing sandwich described in our book was made by taping together two pieces of lantern slide cover glass. Equally good sandwiches can be made of any glass you have handy. Plexiglas or another stiff clear plastic will also work, although these materials will scratch and warp eventually. Another way to make a sandwich is to use a piece of glass for the top and something else—wood, masonite, cardboard, what-have-you—for the bottom.

The printing papers that can be used are of three kinds: each chosen because it doesn't require a darkroom.

Blueprint paper is less used now in engineering and architecture than it once was, but it is still available. Your best source will probably be a local firm specializing in photostats and plan reproduction. Look in the Yellow Pages for Blueprinting Equipment and Supplies. The paper usually comes in rolls approximately a yard wide and several hundred feet long. It costs less than $10.00 a roll.[7]

Studio Proof paper is Kodak's proprietary name for its brand of print-out paper. It is one of the oldest photographic materials still in common use, and Kodak may be the only remaining American manufacturer of such paper. This paper is available—only on order, as a rule—from suppliers of Kodak products. Several similar papers are available from European manufacturers.

Repro-Negative paper is manufactured by Eastman Kodak for the graphic arts industry. It is used by printers, graphic artists, and the designers of electronic circuits. It is available in rolls forty inches wide and wider from Eastman Kodak Graphic Arts Materials dealers; it is not available ordinarily from dealers in Eastman Kodak photographic materials. The dealer who supplies blueprint paper may also be a dealer for these materials; if not, they can direct the buyer to a local source.

The other materials needed can easily be obtained everywhere: string and clothespins (for drying film); sponges, old newspapers, towels,

---

[7]The Workshop for Learning Things (Newton, Massachusetts: Education Development Center, 1973), p. 203. Reprinted by permission.

aprons, (for housekeeping purposes); hydrogen peroxide (to add to the water you dip blueprint paper in); scissors; transparent tape; pencils; a clock; and a bucket or two.

At present, no single school or apparatus supply catalogue lists all of the items needed. We have given some sources for the individual items, but acquiring some of these items may be difficult for certain teachers. The Workshop for Learning Things maintains a limited supply of all the essential materials. A price list from this source follows. To order from the Workshop write:

The Workshop for Learning Things
Education Development Center
55 Chapel Street
Newton, Massachusetts   02160

How to Develop the Film.   The following instructions for developing film were written by a sixth grade class at Frank F. Carr School in Greenfield, New Hampshire. The complete booklet includes instructions for loading a camera and taking pictures.

Before starting the process of developing the pictures you have taken, you must have the proper supplies. The supplies you must have are the following:

1. A long black sack open at both ends.
2. String.
3. A frame.
4. Plastic container.
5. Metal weight.
6. Two-and-one-fourth inch wide lasagna.*
7. Developer solution.
8. Fixer solution.

Put the frame in the black sack first. Then put your film, lasagna, the container, and the metal weight into the sack. You put your hands in the bag and have someone else tie you in so no light can get into the bag.

Find the film with your hands and break the tape off. Unroll the paper until you feel the film.

Try to handle your film on the sides so that you won't get finger prints on it. Unroll the film until you find a piece of tape. You take that off and separate the film and paper. Then put an end of the film into the loop in the lasagna. Then put the film into the lasagna. After this put the rolled up lasagna with the film into the container, put the weight on top of the lasagna, then put the top on the container. Have someone untie your hands.

---

*Lasagna. When we say "lasagna" we do not mean the Italian food. We do mean lasagna is long and you can see through it. You put it on the film when you develop it. We got the name lasagna from our science teacher.

Now take the container out of the bag. Slowly pour your developer through the opening of the container until the container is full. Shake for about thirty seconds every minute for five minutes. After five minutes, pour out developer and put in fresh tap water and agitate for three minutes.

Pour the water out and fill the container with fixer. Do the same for this as you did for the developer. After you have rinsed the fixer out with water, you open the container and take the plastic strip from the film and hang your negatives up to dry.

Printing with Studio Proof Paper. To print a picture from the negative that you have developed, you must have certain things. They are: two pieces of glass taped together at one end (a glass sandwich), studio proof paper (one side is shiny and one side is dull).

To make the real print you are to open the two pieces of glass up and put a square of studio proof paper about the size of your negative in with the shiny side facing up. Then put the negative on it, now close the glass and put it in the sun until the paper turns *purple*. Then take the paper out and that is it.

Warning—Do not leave the studio proof paper out in the sun or it will turn purple and be of no use.

Printing with Blueprint Paper. Place a square of blueprint paper blue side up in your sandwich. Then take your negative and put it on your blueprint paper, dull side up. Close the sandwich. Hold it under the sun. Make sure there are no shadows on your sandwich. Then when the edge of the blueprint paper is almost white, take blueprint paper out of sandwich and dip it in a container with a little hydrogen peroxide and a lot of water for about thirty seconds. You will not get a photo as good as a studio photo but it will be good.

Printing with Repro-Negative Paper. You take the negative and open the glass sandwich, and put the negative in right side up. Then put the repro-negative paper in with the shining side on the negative. Then close the sandwich. Take it where the sun is shining and only expose it three to seven seconds. Then you dip the negative repro-paper into developer (the longer you keep it in the darker it gets). After that put it into water then fixer then water and let it dry. Your black and white picture is printed.[8]

Activity Center

The following materials are needed for the Activity Center:

_____

[8]Sixth Grade Class, Frank Carr School, Greenfield, New Hampshire, *It's So Simple . . . Click and Print* (Springfield: Massachusetts Education Department Center, 1969), pp. 14–21.

1. puppets
2. cardboard TV box
3. mailbox
4. suggestion box
5. address file
6. telephones
7. tape recorder
8. typewriter
9. artificial mike
10. paper
11. magazines
12. newspapers
13. bulletin board

The following activities for children are suggested:

1. *Presenting a puppet play* for the class.
2. *Presenting telephone conversations* alone or with a partner.
3. *Making an address file* with names, addresses, and birthdays.
4. *Typewriting one's own stories* or address cards.
5. *Using a TV box* to present commercials or whole shows.
6. *Conducting an interview* with the tape recorder or artificial mike.
7. *Making a code area* with Morse Code, Indian sign language, or the child's own secret code, and sending messages to be translated.
8. *Writing a suggestion* for the suggestion box—what new materials could be used, a good book to read, a new activity.
9. *Writing a news article* for the room newspaper.
10. *Making a recording* of various sounds in the room and seeing if others can identify them.
11. *Writing a letter* to someone in the room or in the school and mailing it in the class mailbox.
12. *Making a personal tape* telling about himself, but not telling his name; when the tape is played, seeing if anyone can guess who did it.
13. *Putting on charades*—selecting a charade made by others in the class.
14. *Cutting out magazine pictures* to illustrate a story he has written.
15. *Making a map* to find something in the room—having a friend try to find it by following the map.
16. *Writing directions* to find certain places in the school and seeing if someone can follow the written directions.

17. *Making up a game,* writing directions for it, and trying it out on some other children to see if the game works.

Summary

In this chapter, we have addressed ourselves to the question of what to do with the rest of the class while teachers are working with single children or small groups. We suggested a variety of independent activities centered around interests and subjects for choice by each child. Philosophically, the methodology is based upon the idea that children should be responsible for what they have chosen to learn or work on, knowing *always* that the teacher, teacher's aid, or older-aged children are available for help when needed.

The interest centers described were:

1. Book Center
2. Writing Center
3. Science Center
4. Material and Math Center
5. Art Center
6. Talk Center
7. Sensory-Images Center
8. Audio-Visual Center
9. Play Center or "Wendy House"
10. Dream Center
11. Activity Center

6

Children
and Books

Until now we have concentrated on the language experience approach with special emphasis on the practice of key vocabulary as one of the tools of the teacher of those who are learning to read. We have based this presentation on several major points, the most important being:

1. Key vocabulary, as described by Sylvia Ashton-Warner
2. Teacher-pupil dictation, involving psycholinguistic principles of language acquisition
3. The use of writing, as a direct complement of reading, to teach word analysis skills in order to record written expression
4. The instructional use of the alphabet and its necessary inclusion in the language experience approach

This chapter adds the fifth point, the use of published books. The use of these procedures should lead to highly literate pupils. If they are familiar with the spoken word and can compose their own thoughts, they are quite ready to read the printed word. In short, books are now the prime material from which the world and all its ideas are acquired.

We rest firmly on the side of trade books. They have a charm, a point of view. Trade books are published for totally different reasons than are texts. They are aimed at whatever audience is interested in their appeal; they make no claim to satisfy every child in every school from coast to coast, although their publishers are understandably happy when sales are large. They are unique in that they offer the reader a choice; having this choice develops and builds the incentive to read—and to write. Choice necessarily results in intrinsic motivation. Therefore, teachers are not required to do the usual activities to interest learners in a given book; if a child chooses a book, there is a built-in motivation and desire to read it.

Texts, on the other hand, are designed to be sold to every classroom in the nation; therefore, they must fit the entire population. We are not the first to accuse texts of being the dreariest of books available. They aim at the mediocre—they must. Whatever improvements have come about in recent years are a direct result of the increasing criticism of their ineffectiveness; little research supports their use.[1]

Therefore, the logical extension of the practices we have described as the language experience approach is that approach usually called *individualized* or *personalized reading*. Here we stand on firm research ground. We present, perhaps in over-simplified form, the results commonly attributed to this practice; that is, an individualized approach to reading, including the individual conference, produces:

1. Marked and immediate improvement in the attitude towards reading
2. Dramatic increase in the amount of reading within a relatively short time
3. Unusual approval by teachers and children of the individual conference
4. Achievement rarely less, often markedly higher in *any* of the skill areas
5. Improved self-concept

The relative strength of this practice is unmistakable.

What follows is a discussion of the use of library books in general, and their involvement in self-selection individualized reading practices in particular.

Using Library Books in School

There are two major ways through which children are exposed to library books in school. One is hearing the teacher read aloud from such a book; the other is the pupil's choosing a library book to read by herself. It is true

[1]See chapter seven, "What Research Says."

FIGURE 27
Conferencing

that a common family activity at home is for adults to read to children, yet the literature period during the school day is one that we would like to stress.

Too often, teachers feel a compulsion to "cover the material" at all costs—finish the text in the way the manual demands and thus skimp on time spent reading aloud from literary classics. We feel that time spent in hearing good literature is not only time well spent, but actually a better use of time than much of the reading from basal readers. It is true that many teachers are not the best oral readers, but they need only be better oral readers than their pupils. Hearing well-read, beautiful language helps pupils absorb the love of good literature. Furthermore, a study in New York City showed that reading aloud from a selected list of library books in and of itself produced higher reading achievement among second graders than that of other second graders who used identical basal programs but were not read to.[2]

How can we help the teacher to understand some of the ways by which he can charm his class? How is good literature best brought into the curriculum?

---

[2]Dorothy M. Cohen, "The Effect of a Special Program in Literature on the Vocabulary and Reading Achievement of Second-Grade Children in Special Service Schools" (Ed.D.) diss., New York University, 1969).

Reading Aloud to Children

The best and surest way of introducing literature to children is by reading to them. In fact, the more children are read to, the more aware they will become of books and language; the more they are read to, the broader their background becomes. The more they are read to, the more attuned they will become to hearing and eventually imitating good oral reading and good spoken English.

Yet the mere act of reading a good book to children will not guarantee the child's acceptance of it. The teacher must present a story in such a way that the children become completely engrossed in what is being read. This means that the teacher must become a kind of an actor—he must "ham it up!" No one, including children, enjoys listening to someone who reads in a dull monotone. Nor do children get much from hearing a good story if the reading period is held over their heads as a reward for good behavior. When a story must be earned by being good, it loses its intrinsic value. Books can come alive for children only if the teacher is willing to dramatize the story with his voice. The cliché that "practice makes perfect" holds true in reading books to children: the more books a teacher reads to a class the better an oral reader he becomes. Thus, if a teacher wants to be a good reader, he will need to provide plenty of reading practice for himself.

There are many books available that are excellent examples of good children's literature. Libraries have lists of award-winning books (such as winners of the Newberry and Caldecott Awards), and every classroom teacher needs to be familiar with these books as well as many others. There are also many reference catalogues available to help teachers locate books on a specific topic for children of a specific age or interest level.

A Program of Individualized Reading

Because this book stresses a high degree of personalization in reading instruction, our method can be described as being a package composed of key words, language experience or pupil-dictated material, the inclusion of writing at all stages of the reading program, the early introduction of trade book literature, and the acquisition of good children's books in every classroom as well as in the extremely important school library.

When there are approximately five books available for each child whose range of difficulty and the interest are at a specific level, the teacher can do more than just read to the class. He can begin the self-selection program that we call *individualized* or *personalized reading*. This program of reading instruction is unique because it does not impose the content of books upon children in order to teach them to read. In this sense, it is the only program of reading instruction that is not based upon artificial "operant conditioning." It is based upon choice, and the artistry of the teacher rests upon how well he uses the unique choices of the child, whether this involves dictating her thoughts to someone or choosing a book from the classroom supply.

For purposes of identification, let us use the term *individualized reading* as a title for the approach wherein trade books are involved in reading instruction. It is the third phase, following key words and language experience, in a proper reading program.

Moving Children into Books

The goal of any reading approach is to move children into reading published books. The goal advocated in this text is no different, even though the path we describe varies sharply from that of most other programs. We believe all necessary skills can be acquired by using key words, many language experience activities, and, particularly, much independent writing.[3] Thus, we want children to move into library or trade books *of their own choice* as soon as they can deal adequately with the content on the pages. In passing, we might also mention that we have no objection to children's choosing readers to read on their own.

Key vocabulary children acquire early far more sight words on their own than the magic 75 so often cited by proponents of reading programs with imposed content. Thus, such children are ready for the recognition of meaning in symbols—reading. Children in a language experience program move into books of their own choice.

The child's rationale for learning to read is the sudden realization that "I have words in my head!" This awareness comes more readily when it is her own words that she is reading. Transfer of training in reading requires recognizing identical elements in different situations. Saying, watching, tracing, reading back, and writing key words provide a nearly perfect transfer of training. As we said previously, children are reading in order to learn words, rather than learning someone else's words in order to read. A child scans the cards upon which the teacher has printed her own words. She can read them, or they are discarded. She can count them. She

---

[3]Chapter seven, "What Research Says," details the research conducted in favor of the key word approach.

uses them to write stories and letters. Her eyes, ears, fingers converge to perform the full act of reading. This approach could hardly be made more functional.

How soon do children move into reading books of their own choice? Recall that, ideally, there already has been consistent exposure to good books through the class literature period. Beyond this, children can approach the place where books are kept. A table, a set of shelves, a rack, a "ferris wheel"—all can be used to make books available for the exploration of the pupils. We find that books placed so that the covers show attract more pupils than a shelf full of books showing only the spines. Interestingly, book sellers placing their wares in airports, drug stores and supermarkets invariably show books with the cover out; they clearly recognize that there is a magnetic quality about the cover of a book.

Once children can read their own words and phrases, they can be moved into attempts to read either published books or books that others in the class have written. In the beginning, an easy way for the teacher to offer encouragement is by helping the child to find one or more of her own key words in a library book. Once a child finds one of her own words in another setting, the rationale for reading becomes operative; context comes into full bloom. She knows her word—usually an extremely meaningful word; if this word exists in another book, that pregnant meaning tips the child off to what the whole page is about. Even if it does not totally explain the whole page, it aids enough that meaning reaches out and, with a minimum of help, the child can proceed to read.

As part of the procedure, as soon as a child has found her word in a trade book, she should tell the teacher. If the teacher behaves properly, there will be the rejoicing that someone has found a *word,* all by herself! The class is stopped to witness the event. In short, reinforcement of a pleasurable act takes place. The finding is natural, without imposed direction. The child *sought* to find a word, any word, and the seeking is a natural human function.

Once this kind of success is apparent, a rush of activity by most of the other pupils should ensue. We would hope that the teacher is swamped for the rest of the day with children searching, cards in hand, through hundreds of pages of the available books.

The children may want to continue this activity for several days, and they should be encouraged to do so, for activities that involve children in this manner help them move naturally into the world of books. If the teacher will give up a few days of planned instruction to allow the children to experience and act on their excitement about books, the world of reading will have them in its thrall.

FIGURE 28
Browsing in the library corner

Choosing a Book That Is Just Right

Once children have acquired enough ability to read books authored by themselves or others, the teacher can help or even insist that they choose books wisely. At first, the presence of the teacher as a guide is useful; but children actually don't need as much help in choosing books at their level (which is what we mean by choosing wisely) as many teachers think they do. A rule of thumb[4] is a simple way to calm the anxieties of teachers who worry about whether a child find that right book. The teacher can say something like this to the class: "Look over all the books. Pick out one that interests you. Be sure you *like* it. Riffle the pages and choose a page in the middle of the book that has a lot of words on it. Start reading silently. Never mind the story for the moment. As you read, hunt for words you don't know. If you find one, put your thumb down on the table beside the book. If you find another, put your first finger down on the table. Keep going. If you use up all your fingers on that page, *it is too hard.* Put the book back, choose another one you like just as well, and see if it is just right.''

---

[4]Jeannette Veatch, *How to Teach Reading with Children's Books* (New York: Citation Press, 1968).

When teachers are beginning a self-selection, individualized program, they should be quite alert to see that the children's choice of books is based on these two criteria: the child must like the book, and she must find it is just right for her by the "rule of thumb." After a while, children will develop a sense about what books will be easy enough, yet challenging for them.

The truth of the matter is that a given child, from one day to the next, will choose harder or easier books, depending upon herself and her prevailing interests at the time. Children should be encouraged to push themselves some of the time and allowed to relax with something enjoyable a lot of the time. Unfortunately, the old belief that learning must be painful to be good still controls too many teachers. They simple cannot fathom that a child's reading ability will improve if she reads most of the time at her own level. Emmett Betts noted this fact many years ago when he said that too much instructional-level reading will wreck the child's drive to read—and he can hardly be called an individualized reading proponent.[5]

Fitting Children to Books

Whether in instructional or recreational reading, a wise adult can help a child to find a book that is just right for her at that time, in that place. Nancy Larrick has proposed some guidelines that are helpful:

1. Know each child—his interests, anxieties, hopes—and help him find books that are related.
2. Know the books for children by reading dozens and dozens (better hundreds and hundreds).
3. Make hundreds of books available through the school library, the public library, book-club membership, home purchases, etc.
4. Seek guidance in selecting books for specific children through the school librarian, the public librarian, recommended book lists, and current book reviews.
5. Provide the climate for reading and for discussion of what has been read.
6. Provide daily classroom time to read at a leisurely pace.
7. Read aloud to the class every day to introduce new books and poems.
8. Enlist the help of parents so that reading will continue.[6]

The adult should remember that each child will need guidance in learning how to select a book that is just right.

---

[5]Emmett A. Betts, *Foundations of Reading Instruction* (New York: American Book Co., 1957), p. 448.

Getting Started on an Individualized Reading Program

In initiating an individualized program, teachers should select books near the reading abilities of the pupils. If the grade level is three, then there should be a range of books with readability levels a grade or two below and two or three above third grade. A normal spread in an average class is from about four to six grade levels.

As many books as possible should be gathered from all sorts of sources. The county and state libraries have much to offer; all kinds of book clubs offer books that can be purchased with money from the children themselves or from school budgets. Magazines are available, and even adult ones, such as *National Geographic*, are good if their pictures can hold a reader of any age enthralled.

The packaged trade book collection is a new development in the publishing field. Since so many educators do not believe that teachers are capable of asking questions spontaneously from a child-chosen book, these packaged collections have question guides for a teacher to read in order to find out how well a child understands a book. These packaged materials are much better than the standard text materials since they do incorporate a self-choice factor. With them, children are not bombarded with "Tell me the line where . . . " and other banalities that are all to prevalent in the teacher's manuals of basals. These collections are the half-way point between a personalized, noncommercial, individualized program and a planned, sequential, material-centered, traditional program.

The following article, "Individualized Reading Packages," by Lyman Hunt, Jr., Director of the Reading Center of the University of Vermont, and teacher participants in his graduate seminar in reading instruction is an excellent summary of the best of the packaged materials.[7]

An individualized reading program has inherent worth. Teachers who have successfully developed programs agree that most children become deeply committed readers through this approach. As Leland Jacobs of Columbia's Teachers College points out, "the reading act is always an individual matter" regardless of whether or not it is taught in groups. For some time there has been pressure on teachers to individualize instruction. That the vast majority have moved but slightly in the direction of individualized reading is testimony to the fact that it is a difficult undertaking. Problems of organiza-

---

[6]Nancy Larrick, *A Teacher's Guide to Children's Books* (Columbus, Ohio: Charles E. Merrill Publishing Co., 1962), p. xv

[7]Lyman Hunt, Jr., "Individualized Reading Packages," *Scholastic Teacher* (February 1971): pp. 10–12. Reprinted by permission of the journal.

tion, knowledge of materials, and recording and evaluating appear to be obstacles for many teachers.

Admittedly, making reading instruction a personal matter for large groups of students is a large order. Efforts on the part of publishers to assist are, therefore, laudatory. Of particular merit in the programs discussed below are the teacher's guides. Other materials to assist with such essentials as skill development, conferences, enrichment, and record-keeping will encourage teachers to experiment.

Many of the programs reviewed here provide exciting ways to break barriers previously faced by teachers. Published materials of this sort are filling a vital instructional need. One teacher referred to them as "heaven sent." Yet publishers can contribute only so much through printed matter for children and teachers. Then the teacher must take the initiative.

Any teacher who has true command of the conventional textbook program can branch out into individualized reading with the assistance of these materials. Publishers cannot be expected to resolve issues of a favorable classroom environment or the management of housekeeping details. Certainly by providing programs oriented to individualized reading, they've gone about as far as they can go.

Four recently published individualized reading programs are comprehensive. Two others offer supplementary aid to teachers.

One-to-One carries the subtitle "A Practical Individualized Reading Program," and there is much truth to that proclamation. While the program is primarily intended for intermediate grades, there is a great deal for teachers below and above these levels.

Produced by Warren Schloat, *One-to-One* comes in an attractive box which, when opened, is a multislotted file. The bins contain a variety of guides and aids for both student and teacher.

The body of the program consists of guide cards related to 1. a variety of literary forms, and 2. specific books. On the specific book cards are questions based on "Understanding the Reading" and "Going Beyond the Reading." In addition, for the teacher there is a story capsule and information about possible pupil responses to the questions.

An important contribution of *One-to-One* is its emphasis on literary forms and values. The distinction made by author Leland Jacobs between two basic literary forms—discourse ("thought about thought") and nondiscourse ("thought about feeling")—is an essential one.

Not only is the teacher's guide a brief course in the world of literature, but it clearly indicates the mechanics of implementing the program. Teachers who are strongly oriented in the direction of literary values will find *One-to-One* a marvelous assistance. Those needing a literary orientation to strengthen reading instruction will find it an education.

No books accompany the program. While some will find this a disadvantage, it in no way hinders the application of the program. The specific books are among the most popular and are thus readily available from a number of sources. The educational value of *One-to-One* in terms of a sound approach to literature surely compensates for any lack of books. (Prentice-Hall, Educational Book Division, Englewood Cliffs, N.J. 07632.)

Random House Reading Programs are massive in both scope and substance. Six different units—identified by color—contain fifty hard-cover books each. The books are attractive, the variety remarkable, the interest and difficulty range wide. Study cards are pocketed inside the back cover of each book.

The clear and comprehensive teacher's guide, in notebook form, is of true significance. A five-step cycle of book selection, preparation, reading response or conference, and skill activity provides the basis for the program and each step is spelled out in considerable detail. There is a great deal for the pupil to do in addition to reading books. This program, more than any other, presents a model for the essential steps of an individualized reading program. Each step is thoroughly developed. Yet, the guide is intended to suggest rather than prescribe.

The guides and teacher apparatus are more than ample as a starter set for teachers desiring to move toward individualized reading instruction. However, the danger of overkill exists if all aspects of the program are utilized with all students. For example, the prereading and vocabulary cards may prove to be too much of a good thing for high-powered readers. Becoming compulsive about completing all details of this program may be counterproductive. (Random House/Singer School Division, 201 E. 50th St., N.Y., N.Y. 10022).

Invitations to Personal Reading involves ten sets of twenty-five truly fine children's books each, along with accompanying teacher aids, including the significant teacher's resource book. The selected books are not intended to comprise a complete program for individualized reading. Instead, the program has been planned to stimulate children's reading through a sampling of interesting and varied types of books. A cross reference to other good books and a pupil record book are provided. As the program is centered on the best in books for children, a great deal of good advice about children's literature is given to the teacher. Background about selections and suggestions for book conferences, with specific guide questions for each title, are sound and of high quality. A thorough reading of the teacher's guide would prove beneficial for most teachers. For some teachers this program could prove valuable as a starter set for moving toward individualized reading instruction. (Scott, Foresman, Glenview, Ill. 60025.)

Individualized Reading from Scholastic represents a major effort to put the individualized reading concept into a workable package. Certainly every teacher can enhance her [*sic*] understanding of the personal approach to reading instruction by studying the components of this program.

Each of the five kits (for Grades 2–6) is built around a marvelous array of 100 paperbacks. The majority are among the best in children's literature. They span a wide range of interest and difficulty levels. Many teachers above and below the suggested levels will find the program of value.

Conference and activity cards corresponding to each book are arranged alphabetically by title in sturdy file boxes. The conference cards provide short summaries for each book and contain questions which emphasize critical thinking and in-depth responses. The activity cards suggest post-reading enrichment and skill activities. Additional teaching apparatus includes a master work-sheet book with skill-oriented spirit masters, a conference notebook for teacher records, and individual reading logs for student records.

The heart of the program is a high quality teacher's guide, which is clear, concise, and precise. While it presents positive philosophical guidelines to individual reading, the teacher may easily branch out and go beyond. *Individualized Reading from Scholastic* presents a challenge to every teacher by opening doors to reading instruction of the personal sort. (Scholastic Book Services, 904 Sylvan Ave., Englewood Cliffs, N.J. 07632.)

House of Books includes three attractively packaged selections of books from several of the Benefic Press high-interest easy-to-read series. Thus, the range of difficulty levels is wide and the interest appeal high. Other materials, such as record books and guides, are provided to assist the teacher to individualize reading. Yet, the key item, the teacher's guide, is slimmer in size and content than that found in other programs, especially with reference to conference questions and enrichment activities. For the teacher already comfortable with an individualized reading program, *House of Mystery, House of Wonder,* and *House of Adventure* would provide valuable additional sources for lowpowered readers. (Benefic Press, 10300 W. Roosevelt Rd., Westchester, Ill. 60153.)

E & R Development Company, Individualized Reading Cards accompany a host of wonderful titles appropriate for all age groups. The study cards, one each for the student and teacher, provide a variety of vital background information and teacher guidance in a highly succinct manner. There are approximately ten study cards each for the primary, intermediate, and middle-school grade levels. They correspond to some of the best-known books for children. Certainly they can prove a boon to both teacher and student within the framework of individualized reading. As with the *House of Books,* this program will benefit most teachers who have already launched an individualized reading program. (E & R Development Co., Jacksonville, Ill. 62650.)

Once books are acquired, singly or in boxes, they should be arranged for easy access. If a classroom has centers of interest, such as science corners, art corner, and the like, the books should be placed in a corner by themselves. A secluded corner is good. A rug on the floor, a rocker. Ask the children for suggestions. Bring them into such planning. They have ideas, too.

Planning Routines.[8]   Once the book corner is ready, ground rules should be established for its use. The children should help make these rules, although the teacher must indicate boundaries necessary to keep the room smoothly organized. Ground rules worked out to the satisfaction of all will ease classroom management problems. Joint planning sessions not only aid in running an effective reading period, they also help children to feel that they have a part in their own destinies as far as school living is concerned. They themselves help to decide how to use the amount of time wisely, how to follow through on independent activities, how to keep the records required of them, and how to hold conferences with their teacher—in short, they learn how to make decisions so that the whole operation is smooth.

Self-Selection Is Important.   An individualized reading program is a self-selection program. The pupil who selects a book opens a door to a rich, happy experience on her own level. Therefore, this program takes advantage of the inner drives the child possesses to explore, select, and pace herself. The child's ego is enhanced by choosing a book, just as Dr. Barnette found it enhanced by being asked to bring out a favorite word. The same psychological force is at work. When choice is present, the child feels she is a more important person. In this way, a climate which meets the child's emotional needs is established.

First Steps.   There are a number of different ways to begin a self-selection reading program. It is possible to change the whole class over to the program at one time or to change one group at a time. Regardless of the way a teacher decides to begin, he should start by having the pupils make their own selections. An individualized reading program might use sixty to ninety minutes or more of the school day. However, we suggest use of a shorter period of time in the very beginning, during which the teacher and pupils can be engaged in a variety of activities, such as those described in the section on independent activities in the first chapter.

Aspects of Conferencing

Individual conferences will vary from five to ten minutes in length. A daily conference with each child is impossible in a class of normal size, but

---

[8] The material in the following three sections is adapted from an unpublished guide, "Individualizing Your Reading Instruction," prepared for teachers in the Midland Park, New Jersey, school system in 1967 by Virginia Schmidt. Reprinted by permission of the author.

fortunately, each child will not need a daily conference. The conference should be held on a voluntary basis, allowing pupils to sign up when they are ready to participate. A teacher may need to schedule a conference time for the rare reluctant pupil, but this situation usually passes after one or two conference experiences. During the conference, a teacher may ask questions about the book, hear a portion read, check vocabulary, and discover skills that need work. It is from this information gathered in conferences that small groups can be organized to work on specific skills.

There are four aspects of individualized reading that are often referred to in material about teacher-pupil conferences in such self-choice, individualized reading programs:

1. Personal involvement
2. General comprehension or central thought
3. Mechanical problems, vocabulary, elements of a book, etc.
4. Holding an audience

Personal Involvement

The act of choosing a book is as personal a decision as can be made in learning to read; therefore, interest could hardly be higher than in such an act. High interest, in turn, generates an intrinsic motivation to read. This allows the reader to take meaning to the page in order to get meaning *from* the page—the prime consideration of psycholinguistic theory.

For this reason we advocate that the natural beginning of the reading period is to help the pupil become personally involved in the act of choosing a book. This reduces the need to charm, coerce, persuade, or in any way to artifically motivate that child to be interested in reading because motivation is incited by the very act of selecting a book.

Here are some questions to help develop personal involvement in children. Teachers can keep this list handy until it becomes automatic.

What was there about this book that made you pick it up?
Was there some reason you wanted to choose this book to bring to me for your conference?
Why did you choose this book?
Would you like to live as the people in the book lived?
What is different in your life from this story?
What is the same in your life?
Was there a lesson for you or someone you know to be learned in this story?

How did the book make you feel?
What would make you want to read it over again? Or wouldn't you?
What were some of the problems of the characters in this book?
What experiences have you had that were like the ones in the book?

You will note that we are careful not to ask questions that have a one-word answer—especially questions that bring a bland yes or no answer. The skilled teacher will proceed from one question to the next, basing each succeeding question on the answer of the preceding one. This allows movement from the pages of the book to the actual life of the child. Tying reading to living is the best guarantee of continued interest in reading.

General Comprehension

From personal involvement the teacher can move the child into the actual content of the material. Often this is not necessary, since responses to the kind of questions in the preceding section will reveal the extent of the reader's knowledge about the story. But if they don't, here are some questions to get at that element.

What kind of a story is this (fairy tale, sports, adventure)?
Could it really have happened?
Do you always believe everything you read in books?
Did you believe in all that happens in this book?
Did this story take place a long time ago or recently (or when)?
What do you think of this book?
Could you get into an argument about this book? About what?
Did this book make you want to do something? What?
What is the book *really* about?
What do you think made the author get this idea?
What kind of people are in this book? Which ones did you like best? Which ones worried you?
Tell me about the story in a short way.

Mechanical Skills

Inasmuch as word analysis should be taught (and learned) in writing, as described in chapters three and four, there is very little need to spend much time in this *reading* period on work attack skills. If there is a need, the teacher should realize that something is wrong with the way word analysis and attack skills have been developed. The teacher could well need some help to inculcate these skills into writing experiences.

Some mechanical skills can best be covered during reading time. Learning new words, homonyms, antonyms, and the organization of a book can be useful exercises for a few moments during the individual conference. Here are some questions that lead in these directions.

Here is an unusual word. Can you tell me what it means?

If I said (naming an antonym or homonym) would you say this word (point to a word in the book) was the same or opposite in meaning?

Show me the index (table of contents, title page).

How do you find out when the book was printed?

Show me a word you did not know. How did you figure it out (initial sound, blend, rhyming, ending letter)? You did not know this word; let me help you. (Cover up part of it.) Now what do you see? Say it; now here is the whole word. Can you say it?

This word starts like _____, but rhymes with _____. Try it. (In "how-to" books:) Tell me how to make _____? What do you start with?

Holding an Audience with Oral Reading

Children should be asked to read aloud, paying special attention to charming an audience. Too frequently, the practice of reading aloud is used to test the reader's knowledge of the words; this practice will surely discourage the love of reading. No one likes to expose their incompetence. If, as we believe, books are to be the carriers of culture, knowledge, and civilized living, then we teachers must do all we can to make them beloved objects.

Early in their tenure, teachers find out that nothing keeps a classroom of active children (even college students) more quiet than having all reading silently along while one is reading aloud. The impression of intellectual activity is a false one: nothing is happening but the killing of class time—not learning.

Those people who have enjoyed listening to a parent reading aloud at home, or a professional actor reading from a classic in a theatre, or have heard the neighborhood librarian charm the little ones who come for "story hour," can recall with a warm feeling how lovely it was. We believe this should be the prime objective of daily classroom reading—to hold an audience! It highlights the conference; it invigorates the reading; it is a perfect opportunity for a child to "show off" in a healthy way. And what is better for building healthy egos than showing off for a good reason?

The teacher can promote this kind of oral reading by making these suggestions:

Make it sound like you're talking.
Make your voice sound spooky (sad, silly, angry).
Make it exciting!
Pretend you are on TV and you don't want those watching to turn you off.

The teacher can insert brief encouraging remarks in between breaths of the pupil.

You don't say!
That's it!
Aw, really?

Teachers should not hesitate to be a model for their students by reading a selection in their most expressive voice, then asking the pupil to imitate that expression.

Teachers can also incorporate what might be called "value clarification" during a conference situation. For a more detailed description of the process, consult the *Indiana Reading Quarterly* for an article entitled "Value Clarification through Reading."[9]

Some Actual Conferences

To give the teacher an idea about how conferences proceed, we include transcripts of some actual conferences. These are not meant to be the finest conferences ever held; but they did happen, and they may help the novice teacher move away from basal reading into an individualized approach.

---

[9]Florence Sawicki, "Values Clarification through Reading," *Indiana Reading Quarterly* 8 (Winter, 1976).

Dialogue from a Teacher's First Conference
A Charlie Brown Christmas[10] — Grade Three Boy

Teacher: Why did the author write the book?

Peter: He wrote the book to prove how interesting Christmas could be and to make people think about it.

Teacher: Was it worth reading?

Peter: Yes.

Teacher: What did you learn from it?

Peter: Christmas could be fun if you did the same thing that Charlie Brown did. Instead of picking a large tree, he picked a puny tree because it needed his help. He felt sorry for it because it was a little tree among the big trees.

Teacher: Did you enjoy reading the book?

Peter: I enjoyed the book very much.

Teacher: What scene in the book would you like to see in the movies?

Peter: The scene where Linus came out on the stage to talk about Christmas.

Teacher: Would you tell your friends to read this book?

Peter: Yes, because then they'd understand about Christmas. I already told them about the book, but they didn't understand. You have to read it to really understand it.

Teacher: Could this story really happen?

Peter: Yes, it could even happen with my friends, and it would be a good challenge.

Peter's Teacher Reflects.   In the area of mechanical skills, Peter had some difficulty pronouncing words that were unfamiliar to him. Some examples were the words "auditorium" and "psychiatrist." We went over the words together pronouncing one syllable at a time. He still had a problem putting all the syllables together to sound out the word correctly. Once he realized the pronunciation of the word, he told me the meaning of it without any trouble.

---

[10]Charles M. Schultz, *A Charlie Brown Christmas* (New York: World Publishing Company, 1965).

After our discussion about the book itself, I examined Peter on the actual structure of the book, that is, table of contents, title page, index, glossary. He knew all the parts of the book except for the table of contents.

EXCERPTS FROM CONFERENCES

The Grapes of Wrath[11] — Grade Ten Boy

Teacher: Could the story really have happened?

Boy: Possibly.

Teacher: Have you heard people talking about it? What kind of a time was this book written about?

Boy: The Depression—and when people were going out West and in the book, this person got out of prison and tries to build a life out West.

Teacher: You mentioned the Okies were from Oklahoma. That state had some problems in those days. What was this book particularly concerned about?

Boy: The Dust Bowl—it is a real problem. I am not sure how you can prevent it, except by planting shrubbery and grass to hold the dirt down.

Teacher: Have you been out West?

Boy: Yes.

Teacher: Do you think watering is a very practical idea in that country?

Boy: No—but something has to be done. Cattle and agriculture just eat up the grass so that there is nothing to hold the dirt down.

Teacher: Would you say that we, the citizens of this country, should be concerned about it?

Boy: Very much so.

Teacher: But some people say it is none of the government's business who grows what. Have you any ideas about that?

---

[11] John Steinbeck, *The Grapes of Wrath* (New York: Viking Press, 1939).

Boy: Well, I think it *is* the government's business. I guess the people who want to put stuff in the soil are the ones who don't want the government messing around.

Teacher: You have gotten your own ideas on this. Is this book an angry or happy book? And why did you read it?

Boy: Well, I heard about the book and my father asked me to read it. I wanted to read about the hardships because my grand-mother lived in Oklahoma during those days. It was terrible. She even had hardships during the Civil War. But this Dust Bowl was the thing that made her want to move. We came up here to Schenectady.

The Little White House[12] — Grade One Girl

Teacher: The story, you say, is about new chairs. What happened?

Girl: The mother comes in and she has blue and green and red paint.

Teacher: What for?

Girl: To paint their chairs.

Teacher: Why do they want to change the color of their chairs?

Girl: I don't know.

Teacher: There must be some reason—they weren't old chairs.

Girl: No.

Teacher: Does this make sense to you?

Girl: No.

More Fun With Our Friends[13] — Grade One Boy

Teacher: Why did you choose this book?

Boy: Because it had lots of pages in it!

Teacher: That's a good reason. What is the story about?

Boy: The zoo. There are lots of animals in the zoo.

Teacher: Where does the zoo get the animals?

---

[12]Helen M. Robinson, et al., *More Fun With Our Friends* (New York: Scott, Foresman and Company, 1962).

[13]D.H. Russell, et al., *The Little White House* (New York: Ginn and Company, 1966).

Boy: I don't know.

Teacher: Doesn't it say?

Boy: No.

Teacher: Where would you guess?

Boy: The animal catcher gets them—I guess from Africa—lions and tigers and zebras.

Teacher: What does a zebra look like?

Boy: Sort of like a horse with black lines on him.

A Tree Is Nice[14] — Grade Two Girl

(This book is an imaginative conception of the pleasure trees bring.)

Teacher: Let us put the name of the book on the tape.

Girl: *A Tree Is Very Nice.*

Teacher: A tree is what?

Girl: *A Tree Is Nice.*

Teacher: Say the lady's name that wrote it.

Girl: Janice Mary.

Teacher: Not quite.

Girl: Janice May.

Teacher: Udry. The man who made the pictures is Marc Simont. Do you know what this thing means on it—The Caldecott Award Medal. Ever hear of that before?

Girl: That is something that makes the book.

Teacher: No—no, it is much better than that. It means a whole lot of librarians read it and looked at it, and said it had the best pictures of any book that year. What kind of story is it?

Girl: It is about trees.

Teacher: Is it a real story?

Girl: Yes

---

[14]Janice Mary Udry, *A Tree Is Nice,* illustrated by Marc Simont (New York: Harper and Row, 1956). Winner of the 1957 Caldecott Medal.

Teacher: Are you sure? Do they have the trees talking or anything like that?

Girl: No.

Teacher: No. Then you know it is real. Are there any people in it?

Girl: Yes.

Teacher: What do the people do in the story?

Girl: They paint under trees and they sleep under the trees in the shade.

Teacher: So they do things under trees. Where did the name of the story come from?

Girl: (Impatiently) Because trees are nice.

Teacher: Did they prove they were nice?

Girl: Yes.

The Rest of the Class

While the teacher is involved in these activities, the pupil has been busy too.[15] She may have been "lost" in a self-selected book for the entire reading period. On the other hand, the period may have been too long to maintain her interest in the book; attention spans are individual and changeable. What happens to those people who are finished before the period ends? There are many things they can do which can and will hold their interest until the end of the reading period. Here is a list of suggestions that may be useful:

1. Write a book review—a very different task from writing a book report.
2. Illustrate a story or part of a story.
3. Make book jackets.
4. Hold an oral reading time with two or three other pupils.
5. Prepare to tell about a favorite book so that it can be shared with the class.

---

[15]See "Independent Activities," chapter five.

Record Keeping

As a final note, let us say a few words about records. Pupils should be keeping records of their own progress. The form of these records should be simple and in keeping with the ability of the child. They can be made up of various things, such as a vocabulary list and a list of books the child has read. Although each child should keep a complete list of self-chosen books, the teacher will also need records for his own use. Such things that help him to see the pupil's progress and growth, specific needs, and attitude towards reading are some notes worth keeping. There are many ways of setting up such a system; a teacher should select one that is easy and convenient for his particular situation. He might use a card file system or set up notebook with separate pages for each pupil. Entries will vary considerably over time. At the beginning of the program, daily entries may be desired while, later on, entries need only be made weekly or periodically.

The following illustrations are samples of ways in which teachers and children may keep records.

Samples of Children's Records

Name _____	Date _____
Title _____	
Author _____	Book Number _____
Total Pages Read _____	
Comments:	

Date Finished	Title of Book	Author

No.	Title of Book	Author	Date		No. Pages	Comments
			Started	Finished		

Name _____
Day _____
Date _____
Time _____

1. Today during reading I intend to accomplish the following:

2. I accomplished everything I intended to do.   Yes   No
3. I did not accomplish everything because:

Name _____   Pages _____

Date _____

Title/Author _____

Mechanical Skills _____

Critical Reading (Comprehension) _____

_____

Personal Involvement _____

_____

Oral Reading _____

Other _____

_____

Samples of Teacher's Records

Name			
Date	Title	Page	Comments

Students' Names	Week 2/7 Beginning	Week 2/14 Beginning	Week Beginning
1. Mary S.	M (T) W TH F	M T (W) TH F	M T W TH F
2. Joe T.	M T W (TH) F	M (T) W TH F	M T W TH F
3.			
4.			

Name			
Date	Conf. No.	Book	Comments

Name **Leo Urbanek**

TEACHER CHECK LIST FOR INDIVIDUAL CONFERENCE

+	−	?
O.K.	Help!	Not sure

Ability to select a just-right book	9/20⁻	9/22⁻	9/24⁺			
Aspects of conference:						
Personal identification	9/20⁻	9/22?				
Main idea understood	9/20⁻	9/22?	9/25?	10/4 +		
Mechanics:						
New vocabulary	10/1⁺					
Parts of books	10/1⁻	10/5⁻	10/8?	10/11?	10/14⁺	
Uses phonics when necessary	9/20⁺					
Oral reading:						
Holds audience	9/20⁻	9/22⁻	9/26⁻	10/1⁻	10/5?	10/8 +

FIGURE 29

Building a Classroom Library

Unfortunately, not every teacher has an ample supply of books at hand with which to initiate the kind of individualized reading program described in this chapter. There are many ways for a teacher to acquire a sufficient amount of books for his students: borrowing books from a public library, searching in one's cellar or attic, borrowing from another teacher, or even asking students if they have any books at home to lend to the classroom library.

How the Administration Can Help

An example of innovative teaching resulting from creative and supportive administrative policy follows in this section. It illustrates well how teachers can move when they feel free to move. Most teachers feel a bit easier about spreading their wings in unknown fields when the boss says, "Go!"

In some school districts, there are funds set aside for the encouragement of innovative teaching projects. In Midland Park, New Jersey, for example, through the initiative of the Curriculum Committee, teachers were able to obtain the Board of Education's permission to make funds available for those who wanted to try something different with their students. One sixth-grade teacher, Ms. Sharon Patrick, had become very interested in the individualized reading program. Because she had very few books in her room, she decided to try to obtain funds to build a classroom library through the innovative teaching project. She wrote out her plan and presented it; in time, she was allotted eight hundred dollars to carry out her idea.

At the onset of the next school year, she explained the project to her new class. The class became highly enthusiastic about the idea of building a library corner in their classroom. As they talked more about the project, they decided that it would be best to follow some orderly plan. The first step was a discussion of what they should have in their library corner; a list of these items was then made. It included such items as: rug, rocking chair, table, some shelving, card catalogue, book return, plants, lamp, paperback and hard cover books, paperback rack, and magazine rack.

The second step they followed was the selection of the exact items they wanted in their library corner. The children were very much involved in this step, for they helped to decide the kind of rug and books they wanted in the library.

The students held a class meeting to decide about the rug. They first compared different brands and materials. Then they talked about where they should buy the rug. Having decided on a store, the students compared three different rug fabrics to decide which was the best for their purposes. Next, they measured the area of the library corner to determine the correct size. A price listing of the three types of rugs was then obtained, and the children figured out how much each type of rug would cost. Their next problem was to decide on the color of the rug. After noting different colors and their apparent wearability in a classroom situation, they decided on a blue and green oval braid rug.

As you can see, not all of the money was spent on books, because Ms. Patrick and her students felt that they wanted a library corner that added atmosphere to their classroom. (They even decided to purchase a paper Tiffany-styled lampshade to hang over their round table.) It took a few months before all of their desired purchases arrived and were set up in the room.

Throughout the remainder of the school year, this library corner became a very valuable part of the classroom. Students were always using it. This was a place where they could go for a book to read, information concerning a research project, or simply to sit, either in the rocking chair or on the rug, and enjoy their books.

At the end of the school year, Ms. Patrick evaluated her project in terms of the children's and their parents' attitudes concerning the library corner. A questionnaire was devised and completed by both parties. The results were very heart-warming; parents were delighted with the library corner. Many mentioned that they had noticed an increase in the amount of reading their child did during the school year, and that they had noticed a change in their children's attitude towards reading.

The students became quite possessive about their library corner. They even mentioned that they didn't want any other class to have a library corner like theirs—after all, it was all their idea! They also noted that the atmosphere the corner created made them want to go to the shelves to find a book to read. Many said that they had read more books that year than ever before; they said that they enjoyed reading.

We realize that every teacher is not in the same fortunate situation as Ms. Patrick, but we wanted to bring to your attention that books alone, like love alone, are not enough. The arrangement of the books and the way the children are introduced to these books are factors that are just as important as the number of books on the shelves.

Before ending our discussion of this project, let us point out that this library corner began from a teacher's interest in an individualized approach to reading. She became interested through her supervisor, who not only understood the approach but could give specific help in its development. Add to these factors the approval and financial support of administrative forces, and the result was a significant increase in the amount, quality, and speed of reading. This teacher's eyes were open to the fact that a traditional program was simply not adequate to challenge her pupils, and she moved—but not alone.

This is not to say that the only way one can have such a fine library corner is by having lots of money—money helps, but it isn't mandatory. Just as much can be done with second-hand furniture, book contributions, and borrowed books from homes and libraries as Ms. Patrick and her class did with new materials. It is the planning between the teacher and the pupils that lifts the whole activity above the mundane. Enthusiasm cannot help being developed when such team work occurs. In this case as well as in many others, the point is this: the arrangement of books and the atmosphere created by the library corner contributed to an improvement in attitude toward reading so noticeable, that parents were favorably impressed.

Summary

In concluding this chapter about the self-selection and individualized reading program, we will add an outline of the approach. This outline has been developed over the years by many who have worked to help teachers. It sums up the major points that should occur when this type of approach is used.

POINTS ABOUT INDIVIDUALIZED READING

General Comments

Individualized reading is characterized by the following features:

1. It is a method devised to meet individual differences.
2. Its major feature is that children themselves select their own reading materials.
3. It allows children to read and learn at their own rate.
4. It permits teachers to work almost entirely with individuals and small groups.
5. It combines the best elements of recreational reading and one-to-one skill teaching.
6. It does away with groups based upon ability. When groups are organized, they are only temporary, with a single specific purpose.

Advantages of the individualized reading program are:

1. The child proceeds under her own motivation and drive.
2. The child reads at her own pace; slow readers are not publicly stigmatized.

3. Interest is increased because the child reads self-chosen material, resulting in greater enthusiasm for reading and an incentive to read more.
4. The program permits the reading of larger amounts of material than do grouping plans.
5. Each child is taught the skills she needs when she needs them; thus, she realizes the usefulness of skills.
6. The individual conferences promote personal relationships between pupil and teacher.
7. There are increased opportunities to integrate reading with other areas.
8. The psychological effect of the program on the child is healthy and lasting.

Initiating the Program

To initiate the program the teacher should:

1. Examine his own image.
2. Prepare himself professionally.
3. Consult school authorities and parents.
4. Increase his classroom book supply.
5. Arrange the classroom.
6. Plan for independent activities.
7. Establish routines.

Self-Selection of Books

Books can be selected by using the following criteria:

1. Place the responsibility on the child for deciding whether a book is easy enough. Use the "rule of thumb."
2. Determine the reading level of the child by testing.
3. Obtain books that interest children. *Primary-grade children* prefer stories based on familiar settings and experiences—pets, toys, other children like themselves; fairy tales; funny stories about people, animals, happenings; surprise action stories; nonsense stories; rhymes and jingles. *Intermediate-grade children* prefer adventure stories, biographies of great men and women, stories about people in other parts of the world, and imaginative stories about kings and queens. *Upper-grade children* prefer nature and science books, travel books,

club and game stories, mysteries, and semifictional stories.
4. Be sure to provide for the individual reading interests of each child.

Individual Conference

During the five-to-ten minutes of the individual conference the teacher should find out:

1. The child's interest in her book.
2. The main idea and story plot.
3. The mechanics of reading in the book.
4. How well she reads aloud.

The following are specific pointers that may be useful in asking questions:

1. Use questions that are based upon the reading matter, yet help a child relate what she has read to real life.
2. Ask short provocative questions that produce long thoughtful answers.
3. Ask questions that help a pupil to widen her horizons from whatever limited base the reading matter might hold.
4. Frequently begin questions with the words, "why," "what," "when."
5. Ask questions that stretch a child's ability to answer without making the situation unduly embarrassing.
6. Encourage answers that are original with the child and, better yet, new to the teacher.
7. Present questions that show a pupil she has the right to her own opinions, even though she may be asked to consider more than one point of view.
8. Ask questions that drive behind the actual facts presented in the material.
9. Ask questions that have worth in themselves and are not designed to help a pupil guess the answer in the teacher's mind.
10. Give the pupil an opportunity to think before answering. Rapid-fire questioning will disorganize some pupils.

After the conference the teacher should:

1. Keep a record of the child's performance in a card file or notebook.
2. Make group or individual assignments to correct a certain difficulty.
3. Approve a further project related to an interest, or another type of follow-up.

Organization of Groups

The following guidelines may be helpful as a basis to open-ended learning
in groups:

1. Groups are to be organized for single, specific purposes.
2. A group exists for the duration of its purpose and no longer.
3. The activity of a group and the amount of teacher help are determined by the reason for which the group was organized.
4. The reason or purpose of the group must be clearly understood by
   each member, prior to and throughout the group's existence.
5. The reason for the groups must provide a purpose and personal
   challenge for each member.

The categories for grouping are:

1. Ability groups based on:
     tests
     texts
     general achievement or reward.
2. Skill groups based on:
     letter sounds (phonemes)
     word recognition
     oral use of language
     a stage of development.
3. Social groups based on:
     friendship
     interest
     a project
     general cooperation.

7

What Research Says

The research on reading reveals that the majority of attention is devoted to methods in which the pupil is given material to read. All the attendant problems, especially those of motivation and comprehension, are exhaustively explored. It is unfortunate that so little research has examined reading methodology when the material is chosen by the child. Children's own language as the basis for developing reading skills and children's own choice of books as the means to literacy comprise the thrust of this text.

The reasons research is so grossly lopsided in favor of imposed-content methodology are not hard to find. The entire field and those organizations related to it give continuing evidence of their lack of understanding that motivation and comprehension are personal in nature and can only be released under personal circumstances.

We are concerned by the tyranny of textbook learning. Our entire discussion is devoted to helping teachers avoid imposed content and develop a style of teaching that releases content from within the child and sets in motion all the forces of personal communication.

For reading is communication. We do not take meaning from the page unless we bring meaning to the page—this requires life experience. The child who knows certain things is better able to read about them than the child who is ignorant of them; and no amount of word study, work attack skills, or whatever will change that fact. As Frank Smith said, "The information bottleneck is in the brain."[1]

---

[1] Frank Smith, "Some Limitations upon Spoken and Written Language and Its Use," in *Children with Special Needs: Early Development and Education,* eds. H.H. Spicker, N.J. Anastasiow, and W.L. Hodges (Minneapolis: Leadership Training Institute, Special Education, University of Minnesota, 1976), p. 45.

This book has been concerned with two major areas—the language experience approach and individualized reading. Part of the former, key vocabulary as developed by Sylvia Ashton-Warner, although unique with us, was never intended to be an end in itself.

Current developments in the field of psycholinguistics are providing a body of knowledge that cannot help but enhance the use of children's language; this body of knowledge is the language experience approach. Educators' realization of the link between writing and reading is long overdue, and we have tried to help ease the way. Although there has been some research in this area, the important item for the teacher to remember is that a pupil should be helped to write a word he can say—that is, a word he knows. To have to figure out a word that is presented to him, on the questionable grounds that he will recognize it later in another context, is to waste some of the energy a child brings to reading. Children gain the skills of literacy through their own speech and their own communicative needs.

Research on the Language Experience Approach

The British government has come full force in favor of this approach. The Bullock report entitled *Language for Life,*[2] a massive study of two thousand schools, is a comprehensive presentation of the role of language as it relates to learning. Its impact is not decreased by its misrepresentation of another far weaker study[3] which has no controls and makes no judgment (despite its title) about whether a teacher is a good model for formal or informal teaching.

Van Allen began exploring the use of children's natural language as a base for reading instruction in San Diego County in 1961.[4] His research had the effect of providing the teachers involved with "a way of thinking about reading and instructional materials that was a real alternative to the mainstream of instruction."[5]

Later, Vilscek compiled a comprehensive assessment of studies in the field. She states, "The results show a predominant distribution of significant effects favoring language experience instruction. . . . " She has

---

[2]Alan Bullock, *Language for Life* (London: Her Majesty's Stationery Office, 1975).

[3]Neville Bennett, *Teaching Styles and Pupil Progress* (Cambridge, Mass.: Harvard University Press, 1976). For a further discussion of Bennett's work, see Diane Divoky, "The War on Open Classrooms," *Chronicle of Higher Education* 13, No. 22 (1977).

[4]San Diego County Reading Research Project, *Improving Reading Instruction* (San Diego, California: Reading Research Project, 1965). (Topics include: Report of the Reading Study Project, Teacher Inventory of Approaches to the Teaching of Reading, and Analysis of Pupil Data.)

[5]R. Van Allen, *Language Experiences in Communication* (Boston: Houghton Mifflin, 1976).

sought to explain the differences between studies on an objective basis, in terms of "differentiation of operational guidelines for curricula and proposed practices between experimental and control groups within a study and among studies."[6] In other words, she found that some studies that used the term "language experience approach" to describe their method did not, in fact, *practice* that approach.

Research on Key Vocabulary

To date, three research studies concerning key vocabulary have come to the attention of the authors. These studies investigated several hypotheses stemming from Sylvia Ashton-Warner's technique of teaching beginning reading in New Zealand. These hypotheses were based upon the premise that if a teacher could reach into the child's own mind and find the words that had real meaning for him, reading would become a relatively simple and natural task. The studies that follow bear out this premise.

Eleanor Barnette, an author of this book, showed that when children find that teachers are interested in their "power words," their ego concept is enhanced, and their attitude toward reading itself is improved.

Raymond Duquette concluded that the use of key vocabulary improves reading and writing skills and reflects particularly significant gains in word study skills.

Anthol Packer, in a national study of "follow-through children" reported in the *Reading Teacher* that children in a key vocabulary program develop vocabulary that is more meaningful than that contained in basal readers intended for use with the same age levels.

Let us examine these studies in more detail.

The Effects of a Specific Individualized Activity
on the Attitudes toward Reading
of First and Second Grade[7]

The teachers who used key vocabulary found that their children possessed a better self-concept and better attitude toward reading than did the chil-

"Elaín C. Vilscek, "A Decade of Innovations: Approaches to Beginning Reading," Proceedings of the International Reading Association Twelfth Annual Convention (Newark, Delaware: International Reading Association, 1968).

[7]Eleanor A. Barnette, "The Effects of a Specific Individualized Activity on the Attitudes toward Reading in the First and Second Grade" (Ed.D. diss., University of Arizona, 1970), p. 698. Reprinted from *Dissertation Abstracts International* Order No. 70-20 (1970).

dren in the comparison group. These data were obtained by having each child draw a self-portrait which was rated by a panel of judges in the field of art education, and by administering a pictorial differential scale. The pictorial differential scale consisted of a series of twenty-six items to which the child responded by marking either a happy face, sad face, or nonplussed face, whichever face most nearly depicted the child's feelings about the item.

Children were not only permitted, but were encouraged, to start with known words rather than unknown words in the beginning stages of reading. They were not expected to learn irrelevant and extraneous materials that had little or no significance for them, but, rather, they could call upon their immediate or past experiences and give such emotion-packed words as "ghost," "bogeyman," or "pen" (prison). Children who had reluctantly stepped inside the schoolroom only months before were now skipping into the room each morning, crowding around the teacher anxiously awaiting a turn to give their key word.

Each child began to sense his own self-importance. He must be a worthwhile individual, for the teacher not only listened to his word but printed it for him and gave him an opportunity to do something with his special word for the day.

What a marvel it was to watch a child's apathy toward school turn into enthusiasm, reluctance change to eagerness, negativism transform into a positive outlook toward others, hostility disappear, and cooperation appear in its place.

For those readers interested in the design and statistical treatment, we are including part of the description found in the abstract.

The population from which the sample was drawn was composed of 264 first- and second-grade pupils in four schools of the Chandler Public Schools, Chandler, Arizona. The teachers of the pupils in the experimental group were volunteers, and the teachers of the pupils in the control group were randomly selected from the six elementary schools in the district.

Because the groups were intact groups, the experimental design used was the pretest-posttest, nonequivalent, control group design. The two treatment groups consisted of one experimental group and one control group. The instructional programs in the experimental and control groups were similar with the exception of the individualized activity being included in the experimental program. The duration of the experiment was from January 1, 1969, to June 1, 1969.

Data were submitted to analysis of covariance, variance, Pearson produce-moment correlation coefficient, and Kuder-Richardson reliability coefficient, with all hypotheses being tested at the five percent level of significance. A factor analysis of an instrument constructed by the investigator for the purpose of measuring pupils' attitudes toward reading resulted in eleven underlying factors for first-grade children's responses and nine underlying factors for second-grade children's responses.

The major findings of the study were:

1. First-grade children exposed to the specific individualized activity included in the regular reading program developed attitudes which were even more positive than those of first-grade children exposed to only the regular reading program. The results were significant at the 0.05 level.

2. Second-grade children exposed to the individualized activity included in the regular reading program did not increase the positive attitudes toward reading which they already possessed.

3. First-grade children exposed to the individualized activity included in the regular reading program improved their attitudes toward themselves significantly more at the 0.01 level than did the first-grade children exposed to only the regular reading program.

4. Second-grade children exposed to the individualized activity included in the regular reading program had attitudes toward themselves which were no different from second-grade children exposed to only the regular reading program.

5. First-grade children exposed to the individualized activity included in the regular reading program had the same attitudes toward reading regardless of ordinal position in the family.

6. First-grade children exposed to only the regular reading program had the same attitudes toward reading regardless of ordinal position in the family.

An Experimental Study Comparing the Effects of a Specific Program of Sight Vocabulary upon Reading and Writing Achievement of Selected First and Second Grade Children[8]

The results of the post-treatment tests revealed that the experimental first-graders did better on the Stanford Achievement Test than the control children in the areas of word reading, paragraph meaning, and word study skills. These same children performed better in writing samples elicited

[8]Based on Raymond J. Duquette, "An Experimental Study Comparing the Effects of a Specific Program of Sight Vocabulary upon Reading and Writing Achievement of Selected First- and Second-Grade Children" (Ph.D. diss., Arizona State University, 1970), p. 103.

through the use of provocative pictures. These differences in writing, significant at the 0.01 level, were in the number of (1) running words, (2) words spelled correctly, (3) different words, and (4) polysyllabic words. The only advantage of the control group was in vocabulary and that difference was considered negligible.

The experimental second-grade pupils of the same study were considered failures by their teachers at the end of the first grade. They were grouped together for the second grade and at the end of it were compared with those pupils whose teachers considered them as having passed the first grade. The results of the final testing revealed a significant difference at the 0.01 level in word study skills of the Stanford Achievement Test. These findings were in favor of the experimental group. The experimental group also did better in paragraph meaning and were surpassed only in word reading. The results of the analysis of the writing samples revealed the experimental group surpassing the control group in the number of (1) running words, (2) words spelled correctly, and (3) different words. The only advantage that the control group had in writing was in the number of polysyllabic words used.

The findings of the first-grade analysis led the investigator to conclude that the use of key vocabulary and its related activities was better than the basal approach used by the teachers of the control groups. Such practice enhanced both reading and writing abilities of first graders. Its use is also encouraged with those second graders who appear to be behind their classmates after the first grade. Not only do these youngsters catch up to their classmates at the end of the second year but surpass them in phonics, as measured by the word study skills of the Stanford Achievement Test.

Sylvia Ashton-Warner's Key Vocabulary for the Disadvantaged[9]

The language patterns of youngsters in Follow Thru Programs in Arkansas, Florida, Pennsylvania, and Washington State were compared to the language presented in basal readers for the same age groups. Dr. Packer found that the key vocabulary words children ask to learn tend to differ significantly from the vocabulary introduced in popular basal readers. Based on these findings he concluded it reasonable to assume that the children's own vocabulary is more meaningful than the basal reader vocabulary. Further, it may be easier for some children to use their own key

[9]Anthol B. Packer, "Sylvia Ashton-Warner's Key Vocabulary for the Disadvantaged," *Reading Teacher* 23 (March 1970): 559.

words elicited by the Ashton-Warner approach not only in learning to read but also in learning to spell and to express their thoughts in writing.

Selma Wasserman, working with Ashton-Warner while the latter was a visiting professor at Simon Fraser University, developed a project on key vocabulary.[10] Wasserman summarizes:

> The Vancouver Project grew in an attempt to integrate the Key Vocabulary approach to beginning reading instruction in a type of open classroom. Our study of the project had three major concerns. The first was an attempt to obtain some systematic feedback on reading attitudes and language skill development in a group of young children who were introduced to reading through the Key Vocabulary approach. A second area of concern was the promotion of an open classroom model, referred to as an *organic classroom,* as the context in which the project would be carried out. The preparation of Simon Fraser University student teachers was the third major focus. The project classrooms seemed fertile ground in which to train student teachers in current and innovative classroom practices, with input from a variety of university and school resource personnel. What would be the impact on a student's professional development of training in such a laboratory classroom?
>
> In addition to these major concerns, attention was also given to the following questions as they related to the growth and development and learning of young children:
>
> In what ways would the organic classroom contribute to the growth of the young child's positive concept of self?
>
> In what ways would the children benefit from being with the same teacher for a minimum of a two-year period?
>
> What other learning outcomes appear to accrue as a natural concomitant of the organic day program?

Finally, the field project seemed a viable way to further the relationship between the Vancouver School Board and the Simon Fraser University Faculty of Education.

The empirical data from the Vancouver Project tend to support several conclusions.

> Primary children who were introduced to reading through the Key Vocabulary approach did as well on reading achievement tests as those taught in other ways, over a two-year period.
>
> Children who learned to read by the Key Vocabulary approach, in the context of the organic classroom, showed significantly more favorable attitudes toward reading than did the control group children.
>
> Student teachers trained in these "laboratory" classrooms were able to implement organic classrooms in their own teaching with considerable confidence.

---

[10]Selma Wasserman, "Key Vocabulary: Impact on Beginning Reading," *Young Children* 33 (May 1978): 33-38.

FIGURE 30
From library study to life experience

Other conclusions are borne out by the qualitative data.

In spite of the pretraining required, teachers have manifested considerable
interest in the organic program, as evidenced by classroom visits and re-
quests for workshops.

Children in the project classes showed more favorable attitudes toward
school on an incomplete sentence projective test.

A random selection of children's writing indicates that project class children gained facility in expressing their ideas in writing.[11]

Research on Individualized Reading

Research in the field of individualized reading is overwhelmingly in favor
of a self-choice approach. The three references below summarize hun-

---

[11]See also: MaryAnne Hall, *The Language Approach for the Culturally Disadvantaged*
(Newark, Delaware: International Reading Association, 1972); and Russell Stauffer, *Action
Research in L.E.A. Instructional Procedures* (Newark, Delaware: International Reading
Association, 1974).

dreds of studies and emphasize the preponderance of support for this approach. From them we have abstracted five major areas of support which underline its advantages.

1. Marked and immediate improvement in attitude towards reading.
2. Dramatic increase in the amount of reading within a relatively short span of time.
3. Unusual approval by teachers and children of the individual conference.
4. Achievement rarely less, usually markedly higher in any of the skill areas studied.
5. Improved self-concept.

There is some overlap in the research summarized by these investigators. Although some studies are excellent in design and controls, others are not so well done. Nevertheless the preponderance of support for the individualized approach using self-chosen, non-commercial books is unmistakable, regardless of textbook authors' and publishers' opinions.

Richard Thompson, in *Summarizing Research Pertaining to Individualized Reading,*[12] reviewed 51 studies reported in the literature on individualized reading between 1937 and 1971. Of this number, 40 were controlled at least to the extent of using control groups. In 24 cases the results favored the individualized reading group. Only one author reported higher reading achievement for the basal control group. Fifteen researchers reported no significant difference between groups.

Irene Vite, in "The Future of Individualized Reading: Bright and Promising,"[13] compiled studies of 76 groups of children and found that 58 groups favored an individualized reading approach, 5 favored ability grouping, and 13 were neutral.

Frances Seeber, in "Development of the Individualized Reading Movement,"[14] shows that from 1950 to 1964, out of 40 controlled studies, 21 favored individualized reading, 4 favored the basal reader, and 15 were neutral. Forty-four uncontrolled studies during the same time period show that 41 favored individualized reading, none favored the basal reader, and 3 were neutral.

One fact not reported anywhere, however, is the inexpensive nature of a self-selection program of reading instruction. Its main requirement is

---

[12]Richard A. Thompson, *Summarizing Research Pertaining to Individualized Reading.* Unpublished manuscript, 1971. (ERIC Document Reproduction Service No. ED 065 836)
[13]Irene Vite, "The Future of Individualized Reading: Bright and Promising," in *Conference Proceedings: Readings as an Intellectual Activity,* ed. J. Allen Figurel, (Newark, Delaware: International Reading Association, 1963), pp. 232, 325.
[14]Frances Seeber, "Developments of the Individualized Reading Movement," in *Individualized Reading,* ed. Sam Duker (Metuchin, New Jersey: Scarecrow Press, 1969), pp. 387–411.

library books which, of course, are not expendable. The use of the library provides cross-budgeting with instructional supplies, a matter not to be taken lightly in these days of high-priced education.

Figure 31 summarizes the strengths and weaknesses of an individualized reading program. We leave it to you to decide which direction to take with your reading program.

Conclusion

This book has been concerned with the personalization of reading through two approaches. First, we outlined in detail the language experience approach through a unique and innovative idea—key vocabulary. Developed by Sylvia Ashton-Warner in her novel *Spinster* and journal *Teacher,* the practice lends itself remarkably well to American reading instruction and language arts methodology. Second, we presented an individualized reading approach emphasizing the use of trade books and a self-selection methodology. We believe that American teaching methodology is in dire need of this refreshing approach to helping children read and write with their own spontaneous language. In addition, it provides children with the invaluable aid of asking and receiving help from the adults in their lives, both teachers and parents, as they accomplish their academic tasks.

STRENGTHS	WEAKNESSES

STRENGTHS

1. Self-selected books are more likely to satisfy reading interests
2. Greater opportunity for interaction among students in bringing together ideas gained from independent reading
3. Child progresses at his own rate
4. Individual teacher-pupil conferences develop rapport
5. Diminishes competition and comparison; avoids stigma of being in lowest group
6. Each child experiences greater self-worth; takes more initiative
7. Flexible—no ceiling on the learning
8. Some children can be introduced to a much greater variety of reading materials
9. Small groups are formed as needed for specific purposes
10. Through time, teachers should develop greater skill and flexibility in teaching.
11. Some children can be guided in more oral and written expression and in critical thinking
12. Combines well with other methods

WEAKNESSES

1. Inadequate library materials in the schools
2. Danger of insufficient skill development
3. Puts heavy clerical burden on the teacher
4. Difficult to find time for enough individual conferences
5. Young children need much guidance in material selection
6. Hard to judge difficulty of books
7. Is only one of possible ways to accommodate for differences in children
8. Teacher needs to have read many books in children's literature
9. Teacher needs to be able to teach skills as needed
10. Inefficient to teach a skill to an individual that half a dozen need at that time
11. May cultivate habits of carelessness in reading and lack of thoroughness
12. Difficult to administer written seatwork
13. Control (discipline) of room may be more difficult for teacher
14. Teacher must do a good job of interpreting program to the parents

FIGURE 31
Summary of the strengths and weaknesses
of an individualized approach
to teaching reading[15]

[15]Miles V. Zintz, *The Reading Process: The Teacher and the Learner,* 2nd ed. (Dubuque, Iowa: William C. Brown Co., 1975).

Readings

Bibliography

Applegate, Mauree. *Easy in English*. Evanston, Ill.: Row and Peterson & Co., 1962.

Ashton-Warner, Sylvia. *Spinster*. New York: Simon & Schuster, Inc., 1971.

————. *Teacher*. New York: Bantam Books, Inc., 1971.

Barnette, Eleanor A. "The Effects of a Specific Individualized Activity on the Attitude Toward Reading of First and Second Grade." E.D. dissertation, University of Arizona, 1970.

Bennett, Neville. *Teaching Styles and Pupil Progress*. Cambridge, Mass.: Harvard University Press, 1976.

Betts, Emmett A. *Foundations of Reading Instruction*. New York: American Book Pub. Co., 1957.

Bullock, Sir Alan, Chair. *Language for Life*. London: Her Majesty's Stationery Office, Dept. of Education and Science, 1975.

Burrows, Alvina. *They All Want to Write*, 3rd ed. New York: Holt, Rinehart and Winston, 1965.

Chomsky, Carol. "Beginning Reading through Invented Spelling." *Selected Papers from the 1973 New England Kindergarten Conferences*. Cambridge, Mass.: Lesley College, 1973.

Cohen, Dorothy M. "The Effect of a Special Program in Literature on the Vocabulary and Reading Achievement of Second-Grade Children in Special Service Schools." E.D. dissertation, New York University, 1969.

Copeland, Richard W. *How Children Learn Mathematics*, 2nd ed. New York: The Macmillan Co., 1974.

Cramer, Ronald L. "Diagnosing Skills by Analyzing Children's Writing." In *The Reading Teacher* (December 1976), pp. 276–79.

Darrow, Helen Fisher and R. Van Allen. *Independent Activities for Creative Learning*. New York: Teachers College Press, Bureau of Publications, Columbia University, 1961.

Duckworth, Eleanor. "Piaget Rediscovered." In *Readings in Science Education for the Elementary Schools*, eds. Victor & Lerner. New York: The Macmillan Co., 1967.

Duquette, Raymond J. "An Experimental Study Comparing the Effects of a Specific Program of Sight Vocabulary upon Reading and Writing Achievement of Selected First- and Second-Grade Children." Ph.D. dissertation, Arizona State University, 1970.

Gans, Roma. *Common Sense in Teaching Reading*. New York: The Bobbs, Merrill Co., Inc., 1963.

Goodman, Kenneth. "Analysis of Oral Reading Miscues: Applied Psycholinguistics." In *Psycholinguistics and Reading*, ed. Frank Smith. New York: Holt, Rinehart and Winston, 1973, p. 164.

Hall, MaryAnne. *The Language Experience Approach for the Culturally Disadvantaged*. Newark, Dela.: International Reading Association, 1972.

Hartman, Thomas. "The Relationship Among the Ability to Classify Retrieval Time from Semantic Memory and Reading Ability of Elementary School Children." Ph. D. dissertation, Memphis State University, 1977.

Herrick, Virgil and Marcella Nerbovig. *Using Experience Charts with Children*. Columbus, Ohio: Charles E. Merrill Pub. Co., 1976.

Hunt, Lyman, ed. "The Individualized Reading Program: A Guide for Classroom Teaching." In *Proceedings of the International Reading Association,* vol. II, part 3. Newark, Dela.: International Reading Association, 1966.

Joseph, Stephen M., ed. *The Me Nobody Knows: Children's Voices from the Ghetto.* New York: Avon Books, 1972.

Kahl, David H. and Barbara J. Gast. *Learning Centers.* Encino, Calif.: I.C.E.D., 1974.

Koch, Kenneth. *Wishes, Lies, and Dreams: A New Way of Teaching Children to Write Poetry.* New York: Random House, Vintage Books, 1970.

Larrick, Nancy. *A Teacher's Guide to Children's Books.* Columbus, Ohio: Charles E. Merrill Pub. Co., 1963.

Lee, Dorris M. and R. Van Allen. *Learning to Read Through Experience.* New York: Appleton-Century-Crofts, 1963.

Lewis, Richard. *Miracles: Poems by Children of the English-Speaking World.* New York: Simon & Schuster, Inc., 1966.

_____. *Journeys: Prose by Children of the English-Speaking World.* New York: Simon & Schuster, Inc., 1969.

Packer, Athol B. "Sylvia Ashton-Warner's Key Vocabulary for the Disadvantaged." In *The Reading Teacher* 23 (March 1970): 559.

Paul, Rhea. "Invented Spelling in Kindergarten." In *Young Children* 21 (March 1976).

Read, Charles. "Preschool Children's Knowledge of English Phonology." In *Harvard Education Review* 41 (February 1971): 1-34.

Sawicki, Florence. "Value Clarification through Reading." In *Indiana Reading Quarterly* 2 (Winter 1976): 22-26.

Seeber, Frances. "Development of the Individualized Reading Movement." In *Individualized Reading: Readings,* ed. Sam Duker. New Jersey: Scarecrow Press, 1969.

Smith, Frank. *Psycholinguistics and Reading.* New York: Holt, Rinehart and Winston, 1973.

_____. "Some Limitations upon Spoken and Written Language Learning and Its Use." In *Children with Special Needs,* ed. H.H. Spicker, N.J. Anastasiow, and W.L. Hodges. Minneapolis, Minn.: Leadership Training Institute, Special Education, University of Minnesota, 1976.

Smith, Lewis and Glenn Morgan. *Communications Skills through Authorship.* Title III Project. Lewiston, Id.: Lewiston Public Schools, 1973.

Spaulding, Romalda and T. Walter Spaulding. *The Writing Road to Reading.* New York: Whiteside, Inc., and Wm. Morrow and Co., 1962.

Stauffer, Russell. "Action Research in I.E.A." In *Instructional Procedures.* Delaware: University of Delaware, 1974.

_____. *The Language Experience Approach to the Teaching of Reading.* New York: Harper & Row Pub., 1970.

Stewig, John. *Read & Write—Using Children's Literature as a Springboard.* New York: Hawthorne, 1975.

Strickland, Ruth. *The Language Arts in the Elementary School.* Boston: D.C. Heath and Co., 1965.

Thompson, Richard A. *Summarizing Research Pertaining to Individualized Reading.* Unpublished manuscript, ERIC, ED 065 S36, 1971.

Townsend, Agatha. "Workbooks—The Research Story." In *The Reading Teacher* 17 (February 1964): 397.

Van Allen, R. *Attitudes and the Art of Teaching Reading.* Washington, D.C.: National Education Association, Department of Elementary-Kindergarten-Nursery Education, 1965.

_____. *Language Experiences in Communication.* Boston, Mass.: Houghton Mifflin Co., 1976.

Vilscek, Elaine, ed. "Decade of Innovations: Approaches to Beginning Reading." In *Proceedings of the International Reading Association Twelfth Annual Conference*. Newark, Dela.: International Reading Association, 1968.

Vite, Irene. "The Future of Individualized Reading: Bright and Promising." In *Proceedings of the International Reading Association Conference, Reading as an Intellectual Activity*, ed. J. Allen Figurel. Newark, Dela.: International Reading Association, 1963.

References

Dawson, Mildred A. *Language Teaching in Grades 1 and 2*, rev. ed. New York: The World Pub. Co., 1957.

Dunklin, J.T. *Prevention of Failure in First Grade Reading*. New York: Teachers College Press, Bureau of Publications, Columbia University, 1940.

Durrell, Donald. *Improvement of Basic Reading Abilities*. New York: World Pub. Co., 1940, pp. 67-73.

Evans, N.D. "Individualized Reading Program." In *Elementary English* 30 (May 1953): 275 80; also in *Elementary School Journal* 54 (November 1953). 137-39.

Fader, Daniel N. and E.B. McNeil. *Hooked on Books: Program and Proof*. New York: Berkeley Pub. Corp., 1976.

Field, Helen A. *Extensive Individual Reading Versus Class Reading*. Contributions to Education, no. 394. New York: Teachers College Press, Bureau of Publications, Columbia University, 1930. Reprint New York: AMS Press.

Groff, Patrick. "What's New in Language Arts: Oral Language." In *Keeping Up With Elementary Education*. Washington, D.C.: National Education Association, American Association of Elementary-Kindergarten-Nursery Education (Winter 1969-70): 7-10.

Hall, MaryAnne. *Teaching Reading as a Language Experience*, 2nd ed. Columbus, Ohio: Charles E. Merrill Pub. Co., 1964.

Hosking, Elizabeth. "A Study of Children's Vocabulary Reading." M.A. thesis, University of Michigan, 1938.

Howes, Virgil M. *Individualizing Instruction in Reading and Social Studies*. New York: The Macmillan Co., 1970.

Jacobs, Leland B. "Reading on Their Own Means Reading at Their Growing Edges." In *The Reading Teacher* 6 (March 1953): 27-32.

Jones, Daisy M. "An Experiment in Adaptation to Individual Differences." In *Journal of Educational Psychology* 39 (1948): 257-72.

Kaar, Harold. "An Experiment with an Individualized Method of Teaching Reading." In *The Reading Teacher* 7 (February 1954): 174-77.

Keliher, Alice V. *A Critical Study of Homogenous Grouping with a Critique of Measurement as the Basis for Classification*. New York: Teachers College Press, Bureau of Publications, Columbia University, 1931. Reprint New York: AMS Press.

Maib, Frances. "Individualized Reading." In *Elementary English* 29 (February 1952): 84-89.

May, Frank B. *Teaching Language as Communication to Children*. Columbus, Ohio: Charles E. Merrill Pub. Co., 1967.

Meil, Alice, ed. *Individualized Reading Practice*. New York: Teachers College Press, Bureau of Publications, Columbia University, 1958.

Olson, Willard C. *Child Development*. Boston, Mass.: D.C. Heath and Co., 1949.

_____. "Seeking Self-Selection and Pacing in the Use of Books by Children." In *The Packet*, pp. 3-10. Boston: D.C. Heath and Co., Spring, 1952.

Olson, Willard C. and Sarita I. Davis. "The Adaptation of Instruction in Reading to the Growth of Children." In *Educational Method* 20 (1940): 71–79.

Robinson, Ruth. *Why They Love to Learn.* Charlotte, N.C.: Heritage Printers, 1960.

Rogers, Vincent R. *Teaching in the British Primary School.* London: Macmillan, 1970.

Russell, David H. "Evaluation of Pupil Growth in and through Reading." In *Reading in the Elementary School, Forty-Eighth Yearbook,* Part II, chapter 14. National Society for the Study of Education. Chicago, Ill.: University of Chicago Press, 1949.

Sandberg, Herbert, ed. "Individualized Reading." In *Educational Comment.* Toledo, Ohio: University of Toledo, 1966.

Smith, Nila Banton. *Reading Instruction for Today's Children.* Englewood Cliffs, N.J.: Prentice-Hall, Inc., 1963.

Veatch, Jeannette. *How to Teach Reading with Children's Books,* 2nd ed. New York: Citation Press, 1968.

_____. *Individualized Reading for Success in Classrooms.* New London, Conn.: Appleton-Century-Crofts, 1954.

_____. *Individualize Your Reading Program.* New York: G.P. Putnam's Sons, 1959.

_____. *Reading in the Elementary School,* 2nd ed. New York: Ronald Press Co., 1966 (revised 1979).

Wasserman, Selma. "A Study of the Key Vocabulary Approach to Beginning Reading in an Organic Classroom Context." Vancouver, B.C.: Vancouver Board of Education, 1975.

_____. "Key Vocabulary: Impact on Beginning Reading." In *Young Children* 33 (May 1978): 33.

West, Roland. *Individualized Reading Instruction.* New York: Kennikat Press, 1964.

Wollner, Mary H. *Children's Voluntary Reading as an Expression of Individuality.* Contributions to Education, no. 944. New York: Teachers College Press, Bureau of Publications, Columbia University, 1949. Reprint New York: AMS Press.

Zintz, Miles V. *The Reading Process: The Teacher and the Learner,* 2nd ed. Dubuque, Iowa: Wm. Brown and Co., 1975.

Zirbes, Laura. *Practice Exercises and Checks on Silent Reading in the Primary Grades: Report of Experimentation.* New York: Lincoln School of Teachers College Press, Columbia University, 1925.

Index

221